W9-BPJ-119

THE
COMPLETE
BOOK OF
DRESSINGS

PAULETTE MITCHELL

MACMILLAN • USA

MACMILLAN
A Simon & Schuster Macmillan Company
15 Columbus Circle
New York, NY 10023

Copyright © 1995 by Paulette Mitchell
Illustrations copyright © 1995 by Sara Love

All rights reserved. No part of this book may be reproduced or transmitted in any form or by any means, electronic or mechanical, including photocopying, recording, or by any information storage and retrieval system, without permission in writing from the Publisher.

MACMILLAN is a registered trademark of Macmillan, Inc.

Library of Congress Cataloging-in-Publication Data available

ISBN 0-02-052962-7

Manufactured in the United States of America
10 9 8 7 6 5 4 3 2 1

＊＊＊＊＊＊＊＊＊＊＊＊＊＊＊＊＊＊

THIS BOOK IS DEDICATED TO MY BEST

FRIEND, DARRYL, WHO, DURING OUR

FIRST DINNER TOGETHER IN GREENWICH

VILLAGE, MANAGED TO LAUNCH HIS EN-

TIRE SALAD NIÇOISE COMPLETELY INTACT,

BUT UPSIDE DOWN, ONTO THE BRICK

FLOOR OF THAT CHARMING RESTAURANT.

＊＊＊＊＊＊＊＊＊＊＊＊＊＊＊＊＊＊

ACKNOWLEDGMENTS

Thank you to Justin Schwartz, my editor, who made this publication possible.

Accolades to my son, Brett, who very likely ate more salads in one year than any other eleven-year-old boy on this planet.

And to all my friends and cooking-class students—thank you for enjoying my creations.

CONTENTS

INTRODUCTION

THERE WAS A TIME when *salad* meant nothing more than a side dish of tired iceberg lettuce overpowered with large quantities of thick and oily bottled dressing. No longer, thank goodness! This book will reinvent the salads you already prepare and introduce you to a whole new repertoire. With the right dressing, side dish salads will become more lively, and substantial salads will win status on the center of the plate.

In fact, many of my favorite entrées are actually salads—a grilled or broiled chicken breast, a poached salmon steak, or sautéed shrimp served either warm or cold atop a bed of interesting greens and an enticing arrangement of fresh vegetables. This is a meal that's quick to prepare at the end of a busy day, yet elegant enough to serve at a dinner party.

I'm not alone in this passion for salads. Their growing popularity mirrors our growing national concern with lighter eating, fitness, and good nutrition. Today's creative, innovative salads have been elevated to gourmet status, as chefs adopt all sorts of ethnic and exotic ingredients in imaginative, visually impressive, and sophisticated ways. Menus of trendy restaurants from California to New York devote a large portion of their entrée lists to out-of-the-ordinary meal-size salads accented with interesting dressings.

With the incredible array of components now available at greengrocers and supermarkets, we home cooks can now toss together tasty, fresh, and healthful mixtures of greens (or no greens at all!) and fresh herbs married with anything and everything from edible flowers to seafood, poultry, meats, pastas, grains, nuts, legumes, eggs, fruits, grilled vegetables—and the list goes on. But it would be downright sinful to drown these first-rate ingredients in mediocre dressings that overwhelm all those fresh, inviting flavors. A dressing should be the crowning glory of the salad, enhancing but not masking the flavors of the components, complementing the other foods with which it's served, and refreshing the palate with its flavor.

Commercially prepared salad dressings tend to be high in calories, fat, and salt; they often contain artificial colors, flavors, and preservatives as well. Most are quite costly, considering that they are made from relatively inexpensive ingredients. To answer the demands of sophisticated palates, many supermarkets also carry a wide array of "gourmet" dressings that may be a bit more flavorful but also are just as high in calories and loaded with preservatives. Commercial low-fat and fat-free dressings can be unpredictable; many carry a potent smell and taste of vinegar combined with an overkill of sweetness.

The good news is that making salad dressings from scratch enables every home cook to create truly tasty salads of gourmet status. Mixing your own dressing allows you to create state-of-the-art flavors. And you can control the fat, cholesterol, and sodium content, if you wish. The time it takes is minimal, the equipment basic. Most dressings can be easily prepared from readily available ingredients, including a wide choice of fine oils, vinegars, fresh or dried herbs, and other interesting seasonings. The benefits, of course, are fresh and tantalizing flavors, freedom from additives and preservatives, and an endless variety of combinations—to say nothing of saving money!

All of a sudden, your salads will take on star billing rather than just be pushed around the plate. Here are more than a hundred salad dressing recipes to supplement or begin your repertoire. All of them have been tested and retested to achieve balanced and interesting flavor combinations that will bring cheers from even the most demanding diners. By using fresh ingredients whenever possible—freshly squeezed juices, fresh garlic, freshly ground pepper—and top-quality condiments, herbs, and spices, you will find that only one or two tablespoons will be necessary to dress most single-serving salads; the more delicate the greens, the less dressing needed. (A dressing should just lightly coat a salad; if there's a pool at the bottom of your salad bowl, you have too much of a good thing.) Since the yield is half a cup per recipe, you can keep manageable quantities of a wide variety of dressings on hand to provide you with instant and appealing ways to enhance whatever is in your shopping basket.

The choice of dressing for a salad should be given careful consideration, just as you match your jewelry or tie to your outfit. Dressings serve several purposes. In some salads they bind the ingredients; in others they enhance or develop the blend of flavors. Light dressings go best with delicate greens; well-flavored or creamy dressings are best suited to robust and highly flavored greens. Also, don't overlook the possibility of varying temperatures; to add extra interest, warm dressings can accompany chilled or room temperature ingredients, and chilled or room temperature dressings can be served over warm salad components.

The dressings in this book are divided into three categories. Oil and vinegar dressings range from classic vinaigrettes to zesty preparations using a wide variety of oils, vinegars, herbs, and flavorings. Creamy dressings are created with yogurt, buttermilk, sour cream, cottage cheese, and mayonnaise, providing a range of fat content from light to rich and both sweet and herbal flavors. Dressings for fruits are included to inspire fruit salads and fruit desserts. Appendix A ("The Basics") includes recipes for homemade mayonnaise, mustard, crème fraîche, chutney, and basil pesto, all of which can be used alone but also may serve as ingredients for your homemade salad dressings.

Since making a great salad is an ideal opportunity to unleash your creativity and your personal taste, complete salad recipes are not included. On pages 23–24 you will find tips for the selection of salad ingredients. I've included some of my favorite uses for the dressings in the recipe introductions. The listings in appendix B ("Suggestions for Dressing Uses") will also guide you in your creativity. Above all, give your imagination free rein in creating delightful presentations and in combining flavors, textures, and temperatures as you use the dressings as enhancements for all that's fresh and fine in the market.

TIPS FOR SALAD DRESSING SUCCESS

- Since flavoring can be a matter of personal taste, adjust the flavors to suit yourself as you make your salad dressings. Tasted from a spoon, most dressings will seem very strong, so it is best to taste by dipping a salad ingredient, such as a leaf of lettuce, into the dressing. Remember, all dressing ingredients are subject to improvisation!
- Dressings can be made just before using, but most improve in flavor if allowed to stand for about half an hour. When dried herbs are used, this setting time is necessary to soften their texture and bring out their flavor. (This information is included in the "Advance Preparation" tip accompanying each recipe.)
- Shake, stir, or whisk dressings before serving because ingredients often separate after setting.

- Since these dressings do not contain preservatives, their longevity depends on the ingredients they contain. All require refrigeration. For further guidelines, see the "Advance Preparation" tip accompanying each recipe. Often the dressings will be safe to consume for much longer than the time listed, but flavors and textures may become altered over time. It's wise to label your storage container with the name of the dressing and the date it was made.

Here are some guidelines for storage:

- Oil and vinegar dressings made with dry herbs—use within one week
- Oil and vinegar dressings made with fresh herbs—use within four days
- Creamy dressings containing mayonnaise, yogurt, cottage cheese, or whipped cream—use within two days
- Dressings containing fresh juices—use within two days
- Dressings containing fresh fruit—use within one day

SALAD DRESSING INGREDIENTS

When making salad dressings, the secret to success is beginning with quality ingredients. The flavors will be more distinctive, and you're assured of an interesting result with only a minimal number of ingredients. Oil, which carries flavors, creates the foundation for many of the dressings. Fine vinegars, in all of their various colors and tastes, herbs, spices, and the aromatic flavors of ingredients like Dijon mustard, fresh garlic, and gingerroot also play important roles.

Oils

Edible oils most commonly come from vegetables, fruits, and nuts. They vary considerably, each one having its own distinctive color, flavor, aroma, and cooking properties.

The best quality and most flavorful oil comes from the first pressing at a low temperature of a single variety of vegetable, fruit, or nut. Subsequent pressings, using higher temperatures, yield an oil that requires extra refining to remove sediment and eliminate unpleasant odors and tastes. In fact, the refining of highly processed oils can remove so much flavor that the final product loses all its character. This is true of oils labeled "salad" or "vegetable oil," which typically contain mixtures of soy, safflower, sunflower, corn, or peanut oils.

There is no significant difference in the calorie counts of most oils—about one hundred calories per tablespoon. So personally, I use top-quality oils, especially when it comes to olive oil. Olive oil provides flavor along with the fat and calories, allowing the use of less oil to achieve a flavorful end product. At times when I want a flavorless oil, I choose a bland, cold-pressed oil, such as safflower, to allow other flavors in the recipe to predominate.

In addition to varying in flavor, oils also vary in their healthfulness. "Saturated" oils, such as palm oil and other tropical oils, have been shown to contribute to heart disease. Unfortunately, commercially prepared salad dressings often are based on tropical oils, which is another reason to make your own dressings with the more healthful oils such as olive or safflower.

Air, heat, and light can cause oils to turn rancid, so refrigeration is recommended, especially for delicately flavored high-quality oils. Nut oils are particularly prone to turning rancid at room temperature. Some oils, such as olive oil and dressings made from it, may turn cloudy and even solidify when chilled, but they will clear again and liquefy at room temperature. If refrigerated and tightly closed, most oils will keep for six to twelve months. If you use oil sparingly, buy it in small containers so it stays fresh.

Oil and water (or vinegar), which normally separate from each other, are combined in dressings by the formation of an emulsion. When you whisk or shake your salad dressing, the oil droplets are broken down enough to remain temporarily suspended in the water (or vinegar). Many salad dressing recipes will specify that the oil be added very gradually while whisking; however, when working with small quantities, I have found it works just as well to combine all the ingredients at once. Since stabilizers are not added to homemade dressings, the oil will rise to the top and the water will sink as the dressings stand, so it will be necessary to stir or shake the dressings again just before they are used.

The best-quality olive oils are "extra virgin," derived from the first cold pressing of top-quality olives with no chemicals or additives. The oil is full bodied, with a fruity or peppery taste; it has a very low acidity (less than 1 percent). Less expensive "virgin olive oil" comes from the second cold pressings or from the first pressing of olives with a higher acidity (1 to 3 percent). It is usually filtered and medium-green to dark yellow in color, with a flavor that can range from lightly fruity to sweet and nutty. "Pure olive oil" or simply "olive oil" can be made from the second or third pressings of the same olives used to make virgin oil. It is yellow in color, has only a faint taste of olives, and often tastes very oily. "Light olive oil" is pure olive oil with less than 5 percent extra-virgin content. Many consumers select it because of the "light" label, but the only difference between it and pure oil is the milder flavor and color; it contains the same fat and calories as other olive oils. Nutritionally, all varieties of olive oil have the same cholesterol-free and monosaturated fat content and nine calories per gram.

Safflower oil, canola oil, and sunflower oil are very light in taste. They can be used alone or mixed with olive oil to produce a lighter-flavored dressing. These are the oils I recommend for mayonnaise and recipes where blandness is desirable. They are also preferable to olive oil in recipes containing oriental flavorings such as gingerroot, sesame oil, and soy sauce. I have specified the use of safflower oil in these recipes because this is the oil I keep on hand, but canola or sunflower may be substituted.

Flavoring oils have a distinct taste and are used primarily for flavoring rather than for cooking. Since they are highly flavored, a little goes a long way.

- *Nut oils,* such as walnut oil, hazelnut oil, and pistachio oil are well-suited to salads; they provide a delicate balance to bitter leaves like chicory. Nut oils turn rancid quickly, so refrigeration is recommended. Pure nut oils are costly; closely read the label of a less-expensive bottle because it is likely to be a blend containing only a small percentage of nut oil.

- *Chinese or Japanese sesame oil* (dark sesame oil) is made from roasted sesame seeds, giving it an amber color and rich, pungent flavor and aroma. Used in small amounts, it provides a distinctly oriental flavor. Sesame oil made from unroasted seeds is light yellow in color and lacks the characteristic flavor and aroma; it is sometimes called European sesame oil.

- *Infused oils* have been infused with natural extracts, herbs, or spices and are intended for salad dressings or marinades rather than for cooking. Light oils, such as safflower, canola, or sunflower, form a bland background for spices and herbs—the most popular being tarragon, basil, garlic, fennel, mint, marjoram, thyme, rosemary, and savory. These are also becoming popular additions to olive oils. The most favored spices used for infusing are peppercorns, ginger, and chili pepper. Hot oil (sometimes called red oil, hot pepper oil, or chili oil), a Chinese or Japanese oil made from sesame or vegetable oil heated with spicy dried red chili peppers, is usually fiery hot and should be used sparingly. Italian pepper oil—hot red peppers infused in extra-virgin olive oil—is milder.

Tip:

Although herb-flavored oils are readily available in many supermarkets and gourmet shops, you can make your own herb-flavored oil for far less money by following this procedure:

1. Fill a bottle halfway with fresh herb leaves such as basil or sprigs of thyme or rosemary.
2. Fill the bottle with extra-virgin olive oil (or a bland oil such as safflower, canola, or sunflower).
3. Cover and steep for one to two weeks. For a stronger flavor, replace the herbs with fresh ones and store an additional two weeks.
4. If individual leaves have been used, strain the oil. Sprigs may be left in.
5. Store the oil in a cool, dark place.

Vinegars

The piquant tartness in salad dressings is most often provided by the addition of an acid, often in the form of vinegar, a diluted acid. The name *vinegar* comes from the French *vin aigre,* or "sour wine." Like wine, vinegar is produced naturally, through fermentation. Vinegar acts as a natural preservative, slowing the growth of bacteria. More importantly, it has become a valued aromatic complement that can provide flavor in addition to acidity, a wide range of hues, and virtually no calories.

Years ago, most cooks relied on white vinegar alone. Today, however, a wide variety of vinegars are available in even the most basic markets. Since most vinegars keep for up to two years without refrigeration, I suggest keeping an array of your favorites on hand. Buy vinegars in glass bottles rather than plastic, which imparts an adverse flavor. Over time, some vinegars may become cloudy or may develop a sediment; the flavor usually will not be affected. The liquid may be cleared by running it through a paper coffee filter.

In salad dressings, the classic proportion of oil to vinegar is three to one; many cooks insist on even more oil in the mixture, depending on the strength and flavor of both the oil and the vinegar. Personally, I find that high-quality, mild, and flavored vinegars do not require as much oil to achieve a balance of flavors—another advantage of using these vinegars in your lower-fat dressings.

While white, cider, rice, and wine vinegars can be used interchangeably in a pinch, there are flavor and color differences that favor the use of one over the others in different recipes. Their strength or tartness also varies, depending on the amount of acetic acid they contain.

- **Distilled white vinegar,** with a chemical base made directly from grain, is colorless and has a sharp, pure acidic flavor. It adds merely a one-dimensional sourness with no color or flavor notes. In a pinch, it can be substituted for cider or wine vinegar; but you may want to use less of it. (I usually use this vinegar only as a household cleaning acid rather than as a salad dressing ingredient!)
- **Wine vinegars,** the most commonly used acid in salad dressings, are produced from the acetic fermentation of wine; they are mellow in flavor and retain the aroma of the wine from which they are made. Robust red wine vinegar is the better complement to assertive leaves, tomatoes, or salads containing meat. More delicate white wine vinegar is well suited to sweet lettuce salads. Sherry vinegar has a rich body and sweet aftertaste that complements fruit and cheese salads. Other wine vinegars are made from champagne.
- **Balsamic vinegar** (Italian *aceto balsamico*) is an Italian red wine vinegar made by boiling the juice of white Trebbiano grapes in copper pots until it caramelizes. It is then aged for three to thirty years in barrels made from different woods—red oak, chestnut, mulberry, and juniper wood—each one adding a hint of its woody flavor. The result is a vinegar with a heavy, mellow, almost sweet flavor, and a dark color.

Store balsamic vinegar in a cool, dark place for up to six months after it has been opened. Balsamic vinegar is pricey; be aware that cheap imitations are made with the additions of cane sugar, vanilla, licorice, and caramel flavoring—read the labels!

- *Apple cider vinegar,* with a mild, slightly sweet apple flavor and golden brown color, is made from apple pulp and can be cloudy unless filtered.
- *Chinese or Japanese rice vinegars* have a low acid content; Chinese varieties offer a clean acidic taste, while the Japanese version is very mellow and sweet. The colors range from the mildest white to a sweet red and the sweetest purple-black. Rice vinegars are excellent in many dressings and complement oriental dressings flavored with sesame oil. Rice vinegar dressings nicely accent delicate salads of fish, seafood, and mild-flavored vegetables. "Seasoned" white rice vinegar contains rice vinegar, sugar, and salt.
- *Aji-mirin and mirin* are sweetened rice wines for cooking. These products are available in Asian markets and in the gourmet or oriental section of most supermarkets.
- *Malt vinegar,* made from beer rather than wine, has a very distinctive strong and sharp taste, too sharp for most dressings.
- *Herbal vinegars* are made by steeping a single herb or a combination of herbs in white wine vinegar, red wine vinegar, or cider vinegar. Tarragon vinegar is probably the most familiar; however, rosemary, basil, thyme, oregano, chive, mint, and other herbs are also commonly used as flavorings.
- *Fruit vinegars* are made by adding soft fruits and their concentrates to mild vinegars—most often white wine vinegar. Sugar and liqueurs are sometimes added to counteract the acidity; colorings are sometimes added to enhance the appearance. The most common are raspberry, blueberry, cherry, blackberry, and peach; less common is a delicious black currant vinegar. Light and obviously fruity-tasting, fruit vinegars add a special touch to dressings destined for both green and fruit salads and those incorporating poultry or meat.

Another way to add tartness to salads is with citrus juices; some cooks feel that it is better to use citrus juice in the dressing if wine is served with the meal. Lemon juice in place of vinegar is appropriate for Greek salads, Middle Eastern mixtures, and chilled seafood platters. Lime juice is less sharp than lemon; the two can be used interchangeably. For variety, I sometimes use orange juice or grapefruit juice. Freshly squeezed citrus juices are always better than canned, bottled, or frozen ones; reconstituted lemon and lime juices are unacceptable.

Tip:
Although flavored vinegars are readily available in most supermarkets and gourmet shops, making your own is both fun and simple, as well as economical.

HERBAL VINEGAR:

Suggested herbs are chives, tarragon, thyme, rosemary, sage, or basil (purple basil adds a nice hue to the vinegar). Herbal mixtures will also provide interesting flavors. Try rosemary, oregano, fennel, and basil; or sage and thyme.

1. Pour about 1 cup fresh, clean, dry, lightly bruised (by folding and pinching) herbs or ¼ cup crushed garlic or shallot into a bottle or jar that has been sterilized in the dishwasher or in boiling water.
2. In a stainless steel or enamel pot, heat 2 cups of vinegar, preferably white wine vinegar, until hot but not boiling. Bruising the herbs and heating the vinegar will help to release the flavor of the herbs.
3. Pour the hot vinegar over the herbs; cover the jar with a nonmetallic lid.
4. Let the herbs steep at room temperature for about 2 weeks, shaking the bottle occasionally. You will know it's done because it will taste done!
5. Strain the vinegar through several layers of cheesecloth or paper coffee filters. Using a funnel, pour it into a new, sterilized bottle. For an attractive presentation and to identify the flavor, add a fresh herb sprig to the bottle before pouring in the vinegar.
6. Cork or cap the bottle and store it in a cool, dark place for up to 6 months.

FRUIT VINEGAR:

There is no need to buy the prettiest fruit, because it will be thrown out in the final bottling. What is necessary is absolute ripeness to get the most flavor.

1. Pour 3 cups rice vinegar or white wine vinegar into a sterilized jar. Add 1 pound fresh berries or soft ripe fruit. Frozen raspberries will do. Or try something unusual like pears!

2. Seal the jar tightly with a nonmetallic lid and leave it in a cool place for at least 2 weeks, shaking it occasionally.

3. When the vinegar is well flavored (taste to be sure), filter it through several layers of cheesecloth or paper coffee filters, pressing the berries to obtain as much juice as possible.

4. If you want a sweeter flavor, add 3 to 4 tablespoons sugar (or more, to taste) and simmer the vinegar for 5 to 10 minutes.

5. Using a funnel, pour the mixture into sterilized bottles. If you have used berries, you may want to plop in a couple of whole fresh berries for looks!

6. Cork or cap the bottles and store in a cool, dark place for up to 3 months. If a new sediment forms, it is harmless, but may be strained out if you like.

Flavored vinegars can also be made with:

- **Vegetables**—Red bell peppers or onions are especially good—wash and cut into strips, add to a bottle of vinegar, and store in the refrigerator.
- **Hot pepper**—Wash a hot pepper, chop it or cut it into strips, add to a bottle of vinegar, and store in the refrigerator.
- **Horseradish or ginger**—Wash and dry a few pieces of the root, place in a small bottle of vinegar, and store in the refrigerator.

Sweeteners

In dressings, sweeteners are sometimes used to mellow out the flavor of vinegar. In other recipes, the sweetness balances the acidity of tomatoes or the tartness of yogurt. The sweeteners that I have used include brown sugar, honey, maple syrup, and white sugar. Personally, I use these natural products and avoid the use of artificial sweeteners. If you choose to use granulated or liquid sugar substitutes in any of the recipes calling for sweeteners, the amount necessary will vary depending upon the product used. Table-spoon for tablespoon, most are sweeter than sugar; add them to taste.

Ingredients for Smooth, Creamy Texture

Some salad dressings call for the addition of the tangy tartness of cultured dairy products such as yogurt, buttermilk, crème fraîche, cottage cheese, sour cream, or chèvre. Other recipes, including many vinaigrettes, incorporate mayonnaise to add richness and to thicken the texture. While some fruit dressings benefit from tartness, others require the addition of whipping cream for sweetness. These creamy ingredients all create a smooth texture, but their flavors, fat content, and properties vary considerably.

- *Buttermilk,* originally a by-product of butter-making, is now made by culturing milk, usually skim or low-fat, with a lactic acid culture that ferments the milk sugar. Contrary to its name, it does not contain butter. Like yogurt, buttermilk has a tart flavor, but it has a thinner consistency. It is a low-fat product unless whole milk, whole milk solids, or liquid butter has been added to it. Store buttermilk in the refrigerator, where it will keep one to two weeks.
- *Cottage cheese* exhibits the first stage of all cheesemaking, the separation of milk or cream into curds and whey. It is usually slightly salted, but is also available unsalted. Whipped in a blender it will develop a thick creaminess. To add a tartness more similar to sour cream, add a dash of lemon juice.
- *Crème fraîche,* the standard cream in France, is unpasteurized cream that is left to stand, developing a full, slightly sour taste that intensifies over time. Modern methods use pasteurized cream that is cultured. Crème fraîche can be purchased in many supermarket dairy departments; or a low-calorie version can be made at home following the recipe on page 138. Crème fraîche can be used in place of whipped cream or yogurt.
- *Goat cheese,* a tangy, mild cheese made from goat's milk, can be eaten alone or added to dressings and sauces to create a creamy texture. Packaged under the names "chèvre" and "montrachet," the cheese ranges from fresh, soft, cream cheese types with just a faint tartness (which is my choice) to aged chèvre with an undeniable

pungency. Creamy domestic goat cheese is a fine substitute for the more expensive imported brands. Once the packaging is opened, wrap the goat cheese tightly in plastic wrap; store it in the refrigerator for one to two weeks. Do not confuse chèvre with "caprini," Italian goat cheese, which is dried, less creamy, and more acidic than French or domestic goat cheese; it is often marinated.

- *Mayonnaise,* a cold-emulsified sauce traditionally based on egg yolks, can be purchased in several variations. Low-fat, cholesterol-free products are available in most supermarkets; this is the type of mayonnaise I have used in developing the recipes in this book. In most dressing recipes, yogurt can be substituted for mayonnaise.

- *Ricotta cheese* is made from the whey that remains after the production of such cheeses as provolone and mozzarella. The whey is blended with whole or skim milk; ricotta, therefore, is not a true cheese because it is not made from curd. The consistency is like a fine-textured cottage cheese.

- *Sour cream* is pasteurized, homogenized cream that has been cultured with lactic acid bacteria. It contains at least 18 percent milk fat by weight. Sometimes rennet and/or nonfat milk solids are added to give sour cream more body. Slimmer alternatives with true sour cream taste and texture are also available; cholesterol-free sour cream is made with skim milk and vegetable oil. Or, yogurt can be substituted.

- *Whipping cream,* or heavy cream, which contains about 40 percent fat content, is excellent for whipping. The higher the fat content, the easier it is to whip. For the best volume, the bowl, whisk or beaters, and cream should be chilled before whipping. Beat the cream until soft peaks form when the beaters are lifted from the bowl.

- *Yogurt* is simply milk that has been cultured by adding bacteria, followed by a fermentation process. Not all yogurts are the same, however. Some contain active cultures and are more beneficial to the body than yogurts lacking active cultures. Active cultures are necessary for certain recipes, such as Crème Fraîche (page 138). The cultures are destroyed if the yogurt is pasteurized again after the cultures are added. Check the container labeling for "active yogurt cultures" or "living yogurt cultures." Yogurt without active cultures will be labeled "heat treated after culturing." Yogurts also vary in the amount of fat they contain, based upon the type of milk used, ranging from whole milk to nonfat milk. Check the fine print on the label.

If the type of milk is not specified, it is usually whole milk. Some yogurts also contain artificial sweeteners and artificial colorings. Nonfat milk solids, cornstarch, and various additives may be used to improve the texture and stability of the product. "Extra thick and creamy" yogurts work especially well as a substitute for sour cream. Some yogurts contain gelatin, creating a firmer texture that is less creamy. Check the expiration date when buying yogurt: If refrigerated, yogurt with live cultures will keep for about one week beyond that date; pasteurized yogurt will keep even longer. The watery layer that separates in yogurt is simply the whey rising to the top. Stir it back in; it has nothing to do with the age or quality of the yogurt.

Herbs, Spices, and Seeds

Herbs, spices, and seeds will add subtlety and distinction to your salad dressings. And they are an excellent way to enhance flavors when you cut back on fats. Every cuisine has its favorites; use them to lend an ethnic character to your salad creations. Here are a few guidelines.

- Herbs, spices, and seeds should be used with care. It's usually best to use only one at a time if it has a distinctive flavor.
- The amount used requires some discretion and is really a matter of personal taste. Begin by adding a little and increase according to taste, especially for hot flavors like cayenne pepper, chili powder, crushed red pepper, and curry powder.
- The amount of herb added can vary depending on the predominant salad ingredients. For example, a salad of cucumbers will not be overwhelmed by an abundance of dillweed; tomatoes can handle quite a lot of fresh basil; and some fruit salads are improved in taste with an amount of fresh mint that would be overwhelming on another salad.
- Take into account the other dishes on your menu. It is best not to repeat herbs, spices, or seeds in two courses of your meal. Pair a mild-flavored salad with a highly flavored entrée, or vice versa.

- Don't use an herb, spice, or seed you don't care for just because the recipe calls for it. Experiment; substitute one you do like. And when you do like an herb, don't feel the need to stick to it religiously; experiment with thyme or oregano instead of basil on tomatoes or chervil in place of tarragon on a green salad. A change of herbs can make a familiar salad seem new again.
- If you double a salad dressing recipe, do not double the amount of herbs, spices, or seeds. Use just a little more than in the original recipe; then add more to taste.

Dried herbs are available in all supermarkets. Fresh herbs are usually preferable and fortunately are becoming widely available. Other than chives, I have never had success growing herbs inside by my kitchen window. But when the weather permits, fresh herbs are easy to grow outside in a sunny location, even in small pots. In the summer, fresh herbs are also abundantly available at farmers' markets. And, although costly, hydroponically grown fresh herbs are available in some supermarkets year-round.

Fresh herbs, such as basil, mint, dill, and cilantro or fresh parsley, will stay fresh longer if you do not wash them before storage. For the best flavor, try to use them within a few days. Packed loosely in a closed container, they will stay usable for about a week. Some cooks trim the stems, particularly those of herbs that come in bunches, then stand them in a glass or jar filled with about one inch of water and keep them in the refrigerator lightly covered with plastic wrap. Every few days trim half an inch from the bottoms of the stems. Or, wrap the stem ends with a moist paper towel and refrigerate them in a sealed plastic bag.

Most herbs, such as basil, thyme, and rosemary, have tough stems; pinch off the leaves and avoid using the stems. Chop or mince the leaves using kitchen shears, or use a sharp knife on a cutting board. And save a sprig for garnishing your salad!

Some herbs can be dried more successfully than others. Sage, rosemary, thyme, basil, and oregano are quite flavorful in their dried state. Avoid dried parsley, dried chives, and dried cilantro (coriander) because their flavors don't compare to fresh. When purchasing dried herbs, it's a good idea to date the containers. Take an inventory of them annually; those that have lost their color and aroma will not add their distinctive flavors to your recipes. The fresher the dried herbs, the more flavorful they will be. To best preserve dried herbs, do not store them above your stove, but rather in airtight containers in a cool, dark place.

To dry your own herbs, spread finely chopped herbs on paper towels until dry. Then freeze them for up to six months in zip-top plastic bags. (To avoid discoloring, it is best to blanch basil before chopping and freezing.)

When using dried herbs, crush them with your fingers just before adding them to your recipes to help release their full flavor and aroma. If possible, allow dressings containing dried herbs to stand for at least fifteen to thirty minutes before serving to allow the herbs to regain moisture and to bring out their flavor.

In general, one tablespoon of fresh herbs equals one teaspoon of dried herbs, since fresh herbs contain more water and thus take up more volume. This conversion has been provided in recipes that will be successful using dried herbs; in some recipes, only fresh herbs are acceptable.

Spices are the dried parts of aromatic plants that include flowers, fruit, leaves, bark, and roots. Many are available whole or ground; they are often blended to create flavorful mixtures, such as curry powder or chili powder.

The seeds of many herbs and spices from around the world can offer a wealth of flavoring. Many are available both ground and whole; use the form specified in the ingredient lists.

EQUIPMENT FOR MAKING SALAD DRESSINGS

Only minimal equipment is necessary for making your own salad dressings—probably items you already own. I recommend buying the best you can afford for durability, ease of use, and appearance.

- **Blender**—Using a blender is the best method for achieving a smooth consistency in puréed dressings.

- **Bowls**—Since these recipes make $1/2$ cup of dressing, only small bowls are necessary. I prefer stainless steel, ceramic, or glass over plastic, which can retain odors.
- **Citrus juicer**—Because freshly squeezed lemon, lime, orange, and grapefruit juice is preferable to the canned, bottled, or frozen varieties, use a juicer for the best yield.
- **Cutting boards** will come in handy for preparing dressing ingredients. Soft surfaces, such as wooden or molded polyethylene boards, are easier on knives than very hard surfaces.
- **Food processor**—Although I use my food processor daily for many tasks as I cook, it is not necessary for making salad dressings, especially in small quantities. I do use it occasionally for grating Parmesan cheese, and it comes in handy for preparing salad ingredients, such as chopping or slicing onions and shredding cabbage for slaws.
- **Garlic press**—This gadget will not only mince the garlic clove but also will release its juices into your dressings.
- **Graters**—Freshly grated Parmesan cheese is recommended, so purchase a hand-held cheese grater. You can also use a fine grater for citrus rind.
- **Kitchen shears**—These are useful for mincing ingredients, particularly herbs like chives, and for chopping dried fruits and sun-dried tomatoes.
- **Knives**—Good-quality knives will last a lifetime if cared for properly. To keep the blades sharp, buy a sharpening steel and use it often; have your knives professionally sharpened once a year. Do not wash knives in the dishwasher, and store them in a knife block rather than loosely in a drawer.
- **Pepper mill**—Freshly ground pepper is always preferable in making your dressings and for topping your salads at the table. Select a pepper mill with adjustments for fine or coarse grind.
- **Rubber spatula**—A spatula is handy for scraping every bit of your dressing from your mixing bowl or blender as you pour it into your storage container.
- **Shaker**—Most gourmet shops carry salad dressing shaker jars, which can serve as a vessel for mixing as well as storing your oil and vinegar dressings.
- **Storage containers**—Tightly capped containers are a necessity for storing your homemade dressings in the refrigerator. I often use the jelly jars I have saved, but the

most convenient containers for thin dressings are those that have a capped spout in the lid.

- **Wire whisk**—A whisk incorporates dressing ingredients more efficiently than using a spoon. In addition to a medium-size whisk to use in mixing bowls, it also is handy to have a small whisk that can be used in a measuring cup.
- **Zester**—A zester is a kitchen gadget that has a short, flat blade with a beveled end and five small holes. When drawn over the skin of a lemon, lime, or orange, the tool removes long, thin strips of the colored zest. Ideally, do the zesting over the dressing you are preparing to capture the oils, too.

NUTRITIONAL ANALYSES

To guide you in selecting your salad dressing recipes, a nutritional analysis including calories, fat, cholesterol, and sodium accompanies each recipe. Although I usually feel that about two tablespoons of dressing is adequate for most single-serving salads, the sizes of salads varies, and so does everyone's personal preference for proportions. Also, if you toss salads with dressings, a larger quantity is usually required than if you merely drizzle dressings over the top. Therefore the analysis for calories, grams of fat, cholesterol, and sodium is given per tablespoon.

Among the recipes in this book, calories range from three to seventy-seven per tablespoon and fat percentages range from 1 to 82 percent. When analyzed on their own, many dressings seem to contain a high percentage of fat, even if the actual grams of fat are low. For example, one dressing in this book contains just 1.7 grams of fat per tablespoon, yet this accounts for 82 percent of the calories. Also remember: These dressings will not be consumed alone but will become a portion of your entire salad, so the proportion of fat per serving will be reduced. Greens, of course, contain virtually no calories, so even half a teaspoon of oil in a dressing elevates the fat percentage of a simple salad. Since the fat grams per tablespoon remain constant, compare and select recipes based on the grams of fat per tablespoon.

With a balanced selection of ingredients, salads can become the centerpiece of a healthful diet—especially when they are dressed with a moderate amount of a highly flavored dressing. Keep in mind, too, that water can often be substituted for part of the oil; and creamy ingredients can be varied if you wish to reduce the amount of fat in a recipe. Variations can also alter the amount of cholesterol or sodium without changing the calories; some variations can change the entire nutritional analysis.

SALAD BASICS

No longer merely a bowl of limp lettuce, salads today have come into their own. They can be appetizers, first courses, and palate refreshers—even desserts. Often they are the star of the show rather than a supporting player. And when it comes to ingredients these days, you can choose from a cast of thousands. Thanks to America's vast food distribution system, we now have easy access to formerly exotic ingredients—mangoes in Minnesota and fresh strawberries in February. Clearly, salads need not be routine.

Making a meal of a salad has become the quickest, easiest, most versatile and interesting, least fattening, and most nutritious "fast food" available. In addition to fruits and vegetables, we are now adding grains, beans, pasta, lean meats, and poultry to create salads that are rewardingly hearty without being heavy. Salads can also be the perfect destination for leftovers. The elements can be raw or cooked or in combination, and the serving temperature can be chilled, room temperature, or even warm. Salads can be tossed, or they can be "composed," their ingredients arranged with a stylish touch on the plate. Dressings can be tossed with the salad ingredients, or they can be drizzled on top. Salads also can be marinated, allowing you to prepare ingredients in advance to stand in a dressing to absorb and blend the flavors.

Salads can be adapted to make the most of whatever is in season; they can (and should) be served at any time of the year, not just in the summer. Salads can be served in bowls, on plates, or, for variety, they can become the filling for pita bread, soft tortillas, or crispy tortilla shells; some can even be rolled in romaine leaves and eaten as finger food. Few foods offer more visual appeal or more alluring variations than salads; I can't think of any that offer greater possibilities for creativity!

Relax and improvise. There are really no strict rules when it comes to making salads. But here are a few suggestions; use them to inspire your own creativity!

- By varying and contrasting the harmony of flavors, textures, shapes, and colors, you'll achieve the most interesting combinations.
- For a change, mix and match temperatures; serve a warm oil and vinegar dressing over chilled or room temperature ingredients or serve a chilled or room temperature dressing over warm salad components.
- It is not necessary to include a large number of ingredients. Be selective; choose a few items that combine well, with simplicity as your goal.
- When planning preparation time and judging serving sizes, keep in mind that salads including grains, dried beans, pasta, and marinated vegetables can be prepared in advance, travel well, and will be more filling than those concocted of greens alone.
- Vegetables for salads, whether raw or cooked, should be cleaned and refrigerated or cooked shortly before using because exposure to air detracts from their nutritional value and appearance. Don't peel them unless it is necessary; a high concentration of vitamins and minerals are in or near the skin. Many nutrients also can be lost if the vegetables are soaked in water.
- Many raw fruits, such as apples, avocados, bananas, and pears, darken after being cut. Sprinkle the cut surfaces with citrus juice or drizzle them with dressing soon after preparing.
- A good rule for choosing a side salad is to let your entrée be your guide. Do not repeat ingredients. Use your salad as a means of varying textures—a crisp salad with a creamy main course such as a pasta or risotto or a creamy potato salad with cold roasted meats.
- Garnishes will not only add color to your salad but also can provide texture contrast. Crisp garnishes such as croutons, sunflower seeds, or chopped or whole nuts are especially appropriate on soft greens. For firm salads use soft garnishes such as slivers of tomatoes, sliced mushrooms, and grated egg or cheese. Strong-flavored garnishes can easily overpower more subtle flavors; take caution not to overwhelm a delicate salad with ingredients like radishes and caraway seeds.
- Salads will be less likely to wilt and will stay cool if served in a chilled salad bowl. If prepared in advance (except for marinated salads), refrigerate the salad and dressing separately; add the dressing just before serving.

GREENS

- Freshness is imperative! Every ingredient should be of prime quality.
- Pick off any discolored or frayed leaves and store lettuce without washing. Wrap it in a plastic bag and place it in the refrigerator crisper, or store it in a plastic crisper designed for the storage of greens. Properly stored, firm greens will usually keep for about a week; soft-leafed, more delicate greens will keep only a day or two.
- Ideally, wash only the greens you plan to use immediately. When cleaning, never allow greens to soak in water; rinse them under cold running water (or dip them in a pan of water, changing the water if necessary), paying special attention to the base of the leaves where soil may cling. It will be necessary to cut the core out of tight heads of lettuce and cabbage before cleaning. After washing, dry the leaves with paper towels or lightweight kitchen towels, or whirl them in a salad spinner. Excess water on the greens will dilute the flavor of your dressing and will prevent the dressing from adhering.

  If necessary, greens can be washed a couple of hours before using. Refrigerate them in a tightly closed plastic bag with a paper towel in the bottom to absorb any excess moisture. If you need to refrigerate the greens longer than twenty-four hours, also layer paper towels or a thin kitchen towel between the leaves to absorb moisture. The new plastic bags for vegetables, which have tiny air holes to allow air circulation, will also help to extend freshness.
- Serve greens while they are still chilled; most wilt quickly at room temperature.
- If greens are limp, wrap them in a damp paper towel or a lightweight kitchen towel and refrigerate.
- Tear, don't cut, greens to avoid bruising. However, if the leaves are to be shredded, use a chef's knife.
- As a general rule, the darker green the leaves, the more nutritious the salad. Iceberg lettuce, the most common mild lettuce, suffers from a very bland flavor and minimal nutritional benefits compared to other choices that contain vitamin A, vitamin B, vitamin C, potassium, calcium, and iron.
- Use a variety of greens in your salads. Many produce departments now sell a ready-made blend of mixed greens; or create your own combination. Some specialty greens

are available seasonally; others can be found only in specialty markets. The lively variety of tastes they offer makes the search worthwhile!

- For the most tender textures, try "baby greens," from small, immature plants.
- Those greens listed in the "bitter" or "peppery and pungent" categories are commonly used as accents rather than as the basis of an entire salad. Combine them in your salad in this ratio: one part bitter to two parts sweet. The more bitter greens you use, the sweeter your dressing needs to be. You can also add sweet vegetables or fruit, such as grapes, orange sections, or chopped apple, to achieve the desired balance.
- When selecting a dressing for your salad, keep in mind that pungent greens such as romaine, escarole, arugula, and spinach demand robust dressings, while delicate lettuces such as Boston or Bibb are easily overpowered by stronger dressings.
- When dressing a green salad, add the dressing just before serving or the greens will become limp and soggy. Toss the salad in a large bowl, using an up-and-over motion. Use wooden utensils (or your hands) to prevent bruising the leaves.
- Salads taste best cool, rather than served right from the refrigerator.
- Most greens can be used in their uncooked form, but some tough-textured leaves can be softened, or "wilted." Wilting can be done by soaking the leaves (such as cabbage) in boiling water or parboiling them briefly. Leaves more fragile than cabbage—dandelion, chicory, or salad spinach, for example—can be wilted by drenching them with a hot oil and vinegar dressing.

SOFT LETTUCES

Bibb
Boston (butterhead lettuce)
green leaf lettuce
oak leaf lettuce
red leaf lettuce

CHEWY GREENS

mâche (also called corn salad, lamb's lettuce, field salad)—has a nutlike sweetness and mild flavor
radicchio—has a slightly bitter taste and most often a red color

SLIGHTLY CRUNCHY LETTUCES

iceberg (head lettuce)

leaf lettuce

romaine (cos lettuce)

PEPPERY AND PUNGENT

arugula (rocket)—has a spicy, mustardlike flavor; the more mature, the stronger the flavor

bok choy (Chinese mustard cabbage)—use the deep green tops as greens

Chinese cabbage (Napa cabbage, celery cabbage)

mustard greens

sorrel—has a lemony, tart flavor

Swiss chard

watercress

BITTER LETTUCE

Belgian endive—small heads are less bitter

curly endive (chicory)

dandelion greens

escarole (broad leaf endive)

OTHER GREENS

cabbage, green or red

celery leaves

kale—has a nutty flavor

salad spinach—use these smaller, more tender leaves rather than spinach for cooking

savoy cabbage—the mildest form of head cabbage

SALAD INGREDIENTS

When making your salads, foods from this list can be used to add texture, flavor, and visual appeal. Toss them in or use them as garnishes. Or, for variety, eliminate greens entirely and toss an assortment of other items (like a mixture of corn, beans, minced sweet red pepper, and shallot) with your choice of dressing. Create unique combinations. Be nontraditional—for example, potato salad can be made from a combination of steamed new potatoes and chunks of sweet potatoes tossed with an oil and vinegar dressing. Remember, too, that salads are a perfect destination for leftovers.

Cheeses—shredded, grated, crumbled, chunked, or sliced

Croutons—purchase or make your own using the recipe for Herbed Garlic Croutons on page 139

Dried fruits

Edible flowers (be certain they have been grown without pesticides)

Eggs

Fish and shellfish

Fresh herbs—can be tossed with greens in addition to being mixed in dressings

Fruits—fresh is always better than canned; should be ripe for maximum flavor

Grains

Legumes—Canned beans are fine to use; you may want to rinse and drain them well to remove excess salt. The choices are greater, however, if you cook your beans from scratch.

Nuts—whole, chopped, or slivered

Pasta—Be sure to cook the pasta "al dente." If prepared in advance, drain well. To prevent sticking, toss with a little oil, such as olive oil, and chill. Nearly any variety of pasta will do.

Protein sources—including meats, poultry, seafood, and tofu

Seeds

Sprouts

Vegetables—Most vegetables can be used raw in salads. If they are steamed or sautéed, cooking time should be kept to a minimum so that the vegetable's character and nutrients are altered as little as possible. Blanching will intensify the color while retaining the texture of vegetables like pea pods and broccoli florets. Roasting and grilling will add flavor and a different texture. Don't overlook cutting your vegetables into different shapes for variety. With the right technique, they can also be turned into eye-catching decorations for garnishing your salads.

OIL AND
VINEGAR DRESSINGS

AT THE TABLE, salad greens can be brought to life by the simple addition of oil and vinegar. This splendid combination will add flavor and moistness. However, when these two elements are combined in advance and enhanced with other flavoring ingredients, the resulting *vinaigrette* can be far more interesting. The possibilities are infinite by using different oils, vinegars, herbs, and sweeteners in varying proportions.

Regarding oils, if you like a distinct olive oil flavor, use all olive oil. For a subtler version, use part or all safflower or canola oil. Classic proportions of oil to vinegar are three to one, or even four to one. But flavorful, mild vinegar, juice, wine, and even water can be substituted for part of the oil or added to "stretch" a vinaigrette without increasing its fat content.

Many recipes suggest whisking the oil into the vinegar gradually, then adding the remaining ingredients. For half-cup quantities, I think it's usually easiest to whisk together all of the ingredients at once. Sometimes I prepare the vinaigrette in a small jar: Pour in the ingredients, cover the jar tightly, and shake until blended.

Since most of these dressings do not contain dairy products, many of those made with dried herbs will keep in the refrigerator in a tightly closed container for up to a week. Some fresh herbs darken after being minced, however, and their flavor and texture diminish after four days. Tips for advance preparation are provided with each recipe.

Oil and vinegar dressings can be used chilled or at room temperature. Or, for variety, most can be served warm or hot; I especially enjoy the sweet vinaigrettes heated. Heat them briefly after the dressing ingredients have been combined or bring just to the boiling point, taking care not to evaporate the vinegar. Hot dressings can be tossed with fragile leaves such as salad spinach to wilt them. For one of my favorite salads, I drizzle a warm vinaigrette such as Balsamic Vinaigrette (page 29) over artfully arranged, thinly sliced chilled pear wedges and spinach leaves, garnished with chopped pecans and fresh basil leaves.

After storing these vinaigrettes in the refrigerator, the oil and vinegar will separate; simply shake or stir the dressings again before they are used. Dressings made with olive oil will thicken and become cloudy, but they will liquefy after standing for a few minutes at room temperature.

Although we usually think of using oil and vinegar dressings on green salads, don't overlook all of the other possibilities for their use. I use some as marinades for chicken or seafood before broiling. Many are delicious on grains, beans, or pasta.

Oil and vinegar dressings work well for marinated salads; use firm vegetables that are raw, blanched, or steamed. Allow the foods to stand in the dressing for eight hours to permit the flavors to blend; these salads will keep in the refrigerator for two days. To serve, use a slotted spoon to drain off excess dressing; serve on a bed of greens. I often pour a vinaigrette over vegetables such as chunks of new potatoes and sweet potatoes, green beans, chopped sweet red pepper, scallion, and tomatoes. Either warm or chilled, it is a side dish salad that's hard to beat. With the addition of strips of warm or chilled sautéed chicken, it becomes a light entrée. Savory Vinaigrette (page 69) can be the inspiration for an outstanding potato salad. Roasted Sweet Red Pepper Dressing (page 68) is one of my favorites to drizzle, room temperature or warm, over strips of broiled or grilled chicken, also either room temperature or warm, arranged on a bed of greens. And Raspberry-Walnut Vinaigrette (page 66) drizzled over sliced fresh pears is sure to create a sensation at your next dinner party! See appendix B for other inspirations.

APPLE-RASPBERRY VINAIGRETTE

MAKES 1/2 CUP
3 tablespoons frozen apple juice concentrate (undiluted), thawed
3 tablespoons raspberry vinegar
2 tablespoons safflower oil
1 tablespoon honey
1/4 teaspoon poppy seed
Pinch dry mustard powder, or to taste
Dash salt, or to taste

The flavors in this dressing are particularly compatible with sections of grapefruit or slices of avocado on a bed of greens.

In a small bowl, whisk together all ingredients. Taste; adjust seasonings. Whisk or shake before serving.

ADVANCE PREPARATION: This dressing will keep for 2 days in a tightly closed container in the refrigerator.

PER TABLESPOON: CALORIES 50 • FAT 3.5G • CHOL 0 • SODIUM 2MG

APRICOT·SESAME DRESSING

MAKES 1/2 CUP

1 teaspoon cornstarch

1/2 cup apricot nectar

2 tablespoons honey

1 tablespoon raspberry vinegar

1 teaspoon dark sesame oil (see page 6)

1/2 teaspoon minced garlic

1/2 teaspoon minced fresh gingerroot, or to taste

Dash white pepper, or to taste

Pinch crushed red pepper, or to taste

Apricot nectar takes the place of nearly all the oil, making this a very low-fat dressing. Although brief cooking is necessary to thicken it, you'll find it's very quick and easy to prepare. Unless you plan to serve it warm, be sure to plan ahead to allow an hour for cooling. Since the flavor is light and fruity, use this dressing on delicately flavored, soft greens such as Bibb or Boston lettuce. For an extra flavor boost, garnish your salad with toasted sesame seeds to complement the flavor of the sesame oil.

Place the cornstarch in a small saucepan; gradually whisk in the apricot nectar, stirring until smooth. Stir in the honey. Over medium-high heat, stir constantly until the mixture is bubbly. Reduce the heat to medium and continue stirring until the mixture is thickened and clear (less than 1 minute). Remove from the heat; stir in the remaining ingredients.

Transfer the dressing to a jar. Chill, covered, for at least 1 hour. Shake or stir before serving.

ADVANCE PREPARATION: This dressing will keep for 2 days in a tightly closed container in the refrigerator.

PER TABLESPOON: CALORIES 32 • FAT .6G • CHOL 0 • SODIUM 1MG

BALSAMIC VINAIGRETTE

MAKES 1/2 CUP

1/4 cup balsamic vinegar

2 tablespoons extra-virgin olive oil

2 tablespoons water

1 teaspoon Dijon mustard

2 teaspoons minced fresh basil (or 1/4 teaspoon dried basil)

1 teaspoon light brown sugar

1/2 teaspoon minced garlic

1/8 teaspoon freshly ground black pepper, or to taste

Since it contains my favorite vinegar, this is one of my favorite dressings. I love it just as it is, but sometimes for variety I'll replace the basil with a different herb, such as cilantro or tarragon. And sometimes I reduce the calories by using more water and less olive oil.

In a small bowl, whisk together all ingredients, stirring until the brown sugar is dissolved. Taste; adjust seasonings. Whisk or shake before serving.

ADVANCE PREPARATION: If dried basil is used, allow the dressing to stand for 15 to 30 minutes before serving; it will keep for 1 week in a tightly closed container in the refrigerator. If fresh basil is used, the dressing will keep for 4 days.

PER TABLESPOON: CALORIES 40 • FAT 3.4G • CHOL 0 • SODIUM 3MG

BASIC VINAIGRETTE

MAKES 1/2 CUP

1/4 cup red wine vinegar

2 tablespoons freshly squeezed lemon juice

2 tablespoons extra-virgin olive oil

1 teaspoon Dijon mustard

1/2 teaspoon minced garlic

1/8 teaspoon freshly ground black pepper, or to taste

Dash salt, or to taste

This can become your all-purpose basic oil and vinegar dressing. If you prefer, reduce the amount of red wine vinegar and/or lemon juice and increase the quantity of olive oil to suit your own taste.

In a small bowl, whisk together all ingredients. Taste; adjust seasonings. Whisk or shake before serving.

ADVANCE PREPARATION: This dressing will keep for 2 days in a tightly closed container in the refrigerator.

PER TABLESPOON: CALORIES 31 • FAT 3.4G • CHOL 0 • SODIUM 2MG

VARIATIONS:

• add about 1/2 teaspoon dried herbs or 2 teaspoons minced fresh herbs, such as basil, tarragon, or parsley; or add 1 teaspoon fresh dill or 1/4 teaspoon dried dill weed

• add 1/2 hard-cooked egg, chopped finely or forced through a sieve; this is delicious as a dip for artichokes

• add about 1 tablespoon toasted pine nuts, chopped finely

Tip: To squeeze more juice from lemons, limes, or oranges, bring them to room temperature and roll the fruit around on a hard surface, pressing hard with the palm of your hand before cutting or squeezing.

BASIL-SHERRY VINAIGRETTE

MAKES 1/2 CUP

1/4 cup sherry vinegar

1/4 cup extra-virgin olive oil

1 tablespoon finely minced shallot

5 large basil leaves, sliced into a thin chiffonade (see tip), about 1 tablespoon (do not substitute dried basil)

1/8 teaspoon freshly ground black pepper, or to taste

Pinch salt, or to taste

For a Mediterranean treat, try this dressing on a pasta salad with fish and tomatoes.

In a small bowl, whisk together all ingredients. Taste; adjust seasonings. Whisk or shake before serving.

ADVANCE PREPARATION: This dressing will keep for 4 days in a tightly closed container in the refrigerator.

PER TABLESPOON: CALORIES 61 • FAT 6.7G • CHOL 0 • SODIUM .4MG

Tip: Large-leafed herbs, such as basil, and vegetable leaves, such as spinach and lettuce, may be cut into coarse shreds, called a "chiffonade." Stack the leaves on a cutting board and roll the pile tightly. Slice across the roll to make fine or coarse strips, depending on the leaf you are using.

CARIBBEAN DRESSING

MAKES 1/2 CUP

1/4 cup safflower oil

2 tablespoons freshly squeezed lime juice

2 tablespoons orange marmalade

1 tablespoon minced fresh cilantro (do not use dried coriander)

Pinch crushed red pepper, or to taste

Dash salt, or to taste

This sweet, fruity dressing adds life to a chicken salad or tropical fruits.

In a small bowl, whisk together all ingredients. Taste; adjust seasonings. Whisk or shake before serving.

ADVANCE PREPARATION: This dressing will keep for 2 days in a tightly closed container in the refrigerator.

PER TABLESPOON: CALORIES 75 • FAT 6.8G • CHOL 0 • SODIUM 1MG

Tip: Crushed red pepper, or red pepper flakes, are the seeds and flakes of fiery hot peppers; a small amount will go a long way. Refrigerate to preserve the color and flavor.

CHOPPED VEGETABLE VINAIGRETTE

MAKES 1/2 CUP

2 tablespoons red wine vinegar

2 tablespoons extra-virgin olive oil

1/2 teaspoon minced garlic

2 teaspoons minced fresh tarragon (or 1/2 teaspoon dried tarragon)

1/8 teaspoon freshly ground black pepper, or to taste

Dash salt, or to taste

1 small plum tomato, cut into 1/2-inch cubes (about 1/4 cup)

1 tablespoon minced green bell pepper

1 teaspoon capers, drained and rinsed

This zesty dressing is guaranteed to turn a bowl of greens into something extra special. Using this basic recipe, vary the flavor by substituting different herbs such as basil, oregano, or marjoram.

In a small bowl, whisk together the vinegar, oil, garlic, tarragon, pepper, and salt. Stir in the remaining ingredients. Taste; adjust seasonings. Stir before serving.

ADVANCE PREPARATION: If dried herbs are used, allow the dressing to stand for 15 to 30 minutes before serving. Standing will also allow the flavors to blend if fresh herbs are used. This dressing will keep for a day in a tightly closed container in the refrigerator.

PER TABLESPOON: CALORIES 32 • FAT 3.4G • CHOL 0 • SODIUM 19MG

Tip: Avoid using dried garlic powder, which will not lend to your recipes the distinctive flavor, aroma, or healthful benefits of fresh garlic. To make the job of peeling garlic cloves easier, place the flat end of a chef's knife on a garlic clove; using your fist, pound the knife. You will flatten the clove and the skin will separate from the clove inside. Or minced garlic in jars is acceptable; 1/2 teaspoon equals 1 clove of garlic.

CHUNKY MEXICAN SALSA DRESSING

MAKES 1/2 CUP

2 tablespoons tomato juice
or mixed-vegetable juice

1 tablespoon extra-virgin
olive oil

1 tablespoon freshly
squeezed lime juice

1 plum tomato, cut into
1/4-inch cubes

1 tablespoon minced
scallion (green parts)

1 tablespoon minced fresh
cilantro (do not substitute
dried coriander)

1 teaspoon minced
jalapeño pepper (seeds
removed), or more to
taste

1/2 teaspoon minced garlic

1/8 teaspoon freshly
ground black pepper, or
to taste

Few drops hot pepper
sauce, optional

Pinch sugar, optional

To turn lettuce into an entrée salad with personality, place chilled diagonally sliced strips of broiled or grilled chicken on a bed of greens; top with this dressing to add flavor and color. Accompany with Baked Tortilla Chips (page 136). I also like to drizzle this colorful picante dressing over beans or greens to accompany a guacamole omelet or corn chowder.

In a small bowl, whisk together the tomato juice, olive oil, and lime juice. Stir in the remaining ingredients. Taste; adjust seasonings. Stir before serving.

ADVANCE PREPARATION: If possible, allow this dressing to stand, preferably at room temperature, for at least 30 minutes before serving. It will keep for 2 days in a tightly closed container in the refrigerator.

PER TABLESPOON: CALORIES 20 • FAT 1.7G • CHOL 0 • SODIUM 31MG

VARIATION:
• add chopped bell pepper (green, red, yellow, or orange)

Tip: Generally, the smaller the chili pepper, the more fiery the flavor; large and long relates to mild. Since much of the "hotness" comes primarily from the seeds and connecting membranes, remove them for a milder flavor. Be careful to avoid rubbing your eyes, nose, or lips after you have handled chilies because burning can result. Wash your hands, knife, and cutting board in hot soapy water to remove the volatile oil.

CHUTNEY VINAIGRETTE

MAKES 1/2 CUP
1/4 cup chutney (see tip)
2 tablespoons safflower oil
2 tablespoons white rice vinegar
1/4 teaspoon curry powder, or to taste

This sweet-tart dressing with a seductive hint of curry can be made with purchased chutney, or make your own from scratch using the recipe for Mixed Fruit Chutney on page 141.

Place all ingredients in a blender; purée until smooth. Taste; adjust seasonings. Whisk or shake before serving.

ADVANCE PREPARATION: This dressing will keep for up to 4 days in a tightly closed container in the refrigerator.

PER TABLESPOON: CALORIES 50 • FAT 3.4G • CHOL 0 • SODIUM 2MG

Tip: Chutney is a mixture of fruit and/or vegetables cooked with vinegar, sugar, and spices. It can be served alone as a condiment or may be used as an ingredient in other recipes.

CILANTRO VINAIGRETTE

MAKES 1/2 CUP

3 tablespoons safflower oil

3 tablespoons red wine vinegar

2 tablespoons freshly squeezed lemon juice

1/2 jalapeño pepper, ribs and seeds removed, coarsely chopped

1/2 teaspoon Dijon mustard

1/2 teaspoon sugar

1/8 teaspoon freshly ground black pepper, or to taste

Pinch ground cumin

Dash salt, or to taste

1 tablespoon minced fresh cilantro (do not substitute dried coriander)

This one's for cilantro lovers! The herb's unique flavor, prodded by the sizzle of jalapeño pepper, makes this dressing especially good on tomatoes, beans, and poultry.

Place all ingredients except cilantro in a blender; purée until smooth. Stir in the cilantro. Taste; adjust seasonings. Whisk or shake before serving.

ADVANCE PREPARATION: This dressing will keep for up to 2 days in a tightly closed container in the refrigerator.

PER TABLESPOON: CALORIES 47 • FAT 5.1G • CHOL 0 • SODIUM 6MG

Tip: Cilantro, often sold as fresh coriander or Chinese parsley, is found in Vietnamese, Thai, Asian, Indian, and Mexican cuisines. It is especially successful in tomato or rice mixtures and spicy meat, fish, or poultry salads. The dried form is an unacceptable substitution.

CRANBERRY-MAPLE VINAIGRETTE

MAKES 1/2 CUP
3 tablespoons cranberry juice
2 tablespoons red wine vinegar
2 tablespoons pure maple syrup
1 tablespoon safflower oil
1/8 teaspoon freshly ground black pepper, or to taste

 For the best flavor, be sure to use pure maple syrup!

In a small bowl, whisk together all ingredients. Taste; adjust seasonings. Whisk or shake before serving.

ADVANCE PREPARATION: This dressing will keep for up to 1 week in a tightly closed container in the refrigerator.

PER TABLESPOON: CALORIES 19 • FAT 1.7G • CHOL 0 • SODIUM .3MG

DILL VINAIGRETTE

<table>
<tr><td colspan="1">MAKES 1/2 CUP</td></tr>
</table>

MAKES 1/2 CUP
1/4 cup white wine vinegar
1/4 cup extra-virgin olive oil
1 teaspoon Dijon mustard
1 teaspoon minced fresh dill (or 1/4 teaspoon dried dill weed)
1/2 teaspoon minced garlic
Dash freshly ground black pepper, or to taste
Dash salt, or to taste

Use this on salads that include fish or shellfish; the flavor of dill is an especially pleasing complement to seafood.

In a small bowl, whisk together all ingredients. Taste; adjust seasonings. Whisk or shake before serving.

ADVANCE PREPARATION: If dried dill weed is used, allow the dressing to stand for 15 to 30 minutes before serving; it will keep for 1 week in a tightly closed container in the refrigerator. If fresh dill is used, the dressing will keep for 4 days.

PER TABLESPOON: CALORIES **61** • FAT **6.7G** • CHOL **0** • SODIUM **2MG**

Tip: Dill, or dill weed, is an aromatic herb with a lemony taste. It blends well with fish, shellfish, chicken, eggs, cucumber, tomatoes, potatoes, and yogurt. When using fresh dill weed, use scissors to cut the feathery dill tips. Dried dill is acceptable, but use it in moderation.

FAT-FREE VINAIGRETTE

MAKES 1/2 CUP

1/4 cup tomato juice or mixed-vegetable juice

2 tablespoons red wine vinegar

2 tablespoons freshly squeezed lemon juice

1 teaspoon Dijon mustard

1/2 teaspoon Worcestershire sauce

1/2 teaspoon minced garlic

1/8 teaspoon freshly ground black pepper, or to taste

Pinch salt, or to taste

This virtuous dressing is great as is, but if you prefer, add herbs such as basil, oregano, or rosemary (about 1 tablespoon minced fresh or about 1/2 teaspoon dried).

In a small bowl, whisk together all ingredients. Taste; adjust seasonings. Whisk or shake before serving.

ADVANCE PREPARATION: This dressing will keep for 2 days in a tightly closed container in the refrigerator.

PER TABLESPOON: CALORIES 3 • FAT 0 • CHOL 0 • SODIUM 6MG

GARDEN SALAD DRESSING

MAKES 1/2 CUP
2 tablespoons chopped celery
2 tablespoons chopped carrot
2 tablespoons minced parsley
1 scallion (green parts), chopped
3 tablespoons white wine vinegar
3 tablespoons extra-virgin olive oil
1 tablespoon water
1/2 teaspoon minced garlic
1/4 teaspoon dry mustard powder
1/8 teaspoon freshly ground black pepper, or to taste

This delicious verdant dressing will add color to your salad and a hearty flavor that will complement any greens or chunks of potato; or use it as a dip for fresh vegetables.

Place all ingredients in a blender; purée until smooth. Taste; adjust seasonings. Chill. Stir before serving.

ADVANCE PREPARATION: This dressing will keep for 2 days in a tightly closed container in the refrigerator. After standing, it thickens; thin by stirring in water.

PER TABLESPOON: CALORIES 47 • FAT 5G • CHOL 0 • SODIUM 3MG

GINGER-SOY VINAIGRETTE

<table>
<tr><td>MAKES 1/2 CUP</td></tr>
</table>

1/3 cup white rice vinegar

2 tablespoons safflower oil

1 tablespoon low-sodium
soy sauce

2 teaspoons toasted sesame
seeds (see tip)

1 teaspoon Dijon mustard

1 teaspoon minced fresh
gingerroot, or to taste

1/2 teaspoon minced garlic

1/4 teaspoon freshly
ground black pepper, or
to taste

toss this with a mixture of garbanzo beans, sliced mushrooms, cubed tomatoes, diced green bell pepper, and minced parsley. Refrigerated in a covered bowl, it will keep for 3 or 4 days. Because it contains no dairy products, this is a good picnic salad. Or, for an ethnic mélange, serve this dressing warmed over baby greens, garnished with warmed balls of mild chèvre rolled in toasted sesame seeds.

In a small bowl, whisk together all ingredients. Taste; adjust seasonings. Stir or shake before serving.

ADVANCE PREPARATION: This dressing will keep for 1 week in a tightly closed container in the refrigerator.

PER TABLESPOON: CALORIES 37 • FAT 3.8G • CHOL 0 • SODIUM 77MG

Tip: The nuttiness of many seeds, such as sesame seeds, is enhanced by toasting. The simplest method is to toast them in a dry nonstick skillet over medium to medium-high heat on the stove for 3 to 5 minutes. Toss constantly and watch closely, removing them from the pan when they are lightly browned. If you prefer, the seeds can be spread on an ungreased baking sheet in a 350°F. oven. Shake the pan or stir occasionally until they are lightly browned, about 10 minutes. It takes the same amount of time to toast 1 tablespoon or 1/2 cup, so toast extra seeds and store them. Because they contain oil, sesame seeds become rancid quickly at room temperature; refrigerate them in an airtight container both before and after toasting.

GINGERED LIME VINAIGRETTE

MAKES 1/2 CUP
1/4 cup freshly squeezed lime juice
1 tablespoon safflower oil
3 tablespoons honey
1/2 teaspoon minced fresh gingerroot, or to taste

Since this dressing draws on Asian flavors, I like to add Chinese pea pods and bean sprouts to the salad greens to carry out the ethnic theme. For a quick-to-prepare Lime Vinaigrette, just omit the gingerroot.

In a small bowl, whisk together all ingredients. Taste; adjust seasonings. Whisk or shake before serving.

ADVANCE PREPARATION: This dressing will keep for 2 days in a tightly closed container in the refrigerator.

PER TABLESPOON: CALORIES 42 • FAT 1.7G • CHOL 0 • SODIUM .5MG

Tip: If honey crystallizes, stand the opened jar in a pan of hot water until it liquefies; or microwave 1 cup of honey on high for 2 minutes or until the crystals dissolve, stirring every 30 seconds.

GINGERED PLUM VINAIGRETTE

MAKES 1/2 CUP

1/2 teaspoon grated orange rind

1/4 cup freshly squeezed orange juice

2 tablespoons Chinese plum sauce

1 tablespoon freshly squeezed lime juice

1 tablespoon white rice vinegar

1/2 teaspoon minced fresh gingerroot, or to taste

1/2 teaspoon Dijon mustard

1/2 teaspoon minced garlic

Pinch crushed red pepper, or to taste

This sweet, low-fat dressing can turn leftovers into something special when drizzled over greens topped with chicken, fish, shellfish, or fruit.

In a small bowl, whisk together all ingredients. Taste; adjust seasonings. Whisk or shake before serving.

ADVANCE PREPARATION: This dressing will keep for 2 days in a tightly closed container in the refrigerator.

PER TABLESPOON: CALORIES 17 • FAT .02G • CHOL 0 • SODIUM 2MG

Tip: Chinese plum sauce is a thick sauce made from plums, apricots, chilies, vinegar, and spices. Look for it in the oriental section of most supermarkets; store it in the refrigerator after opening.

GRAPEFRUIT VINAIGRETTE

MAKES 1/2 CUP

1/4 cup grapefruit juice

1 tablespoon extra-virgin olive oil

2 teaspoons raspberry vinegar

1 teaspoon minced chives (do not substitute dried chives; if unavailable, substitute minced scallion greens)

1/2 teaspoon sugar, or to taste

1/8 teaspoon freshly ground black pepper, or to taste

The tart, piquant character of this citrus dressing keeps it light and refreshing. If you're looking for a first course to awaken the palate, just drizzle it over an artful arrangement of grapefruit and orange sections.

In a small bowl, whisk together all ingredients. Taste; adjust seasonings. Whisk or shake before serving.

ADVANCE PREPARATION: This dressing will keep for 2 days in a tightly closed container in the refrigerator.

PER TABLESPOON: CALORIES 19 • FAT 1.7G • CHOL 0 • SODIUM .1MG

GREEN FRENCH DRESSING

<table>
<tr><td>

MAKES 1/2 CUP

1/4 cup plus 1 tablespoon
extra-virgin olive oil

1/4 cup white wine vinegar

1/3 cup loosely packed
fresh parsley sprigs

1/2 teaspoon Dijon
mustard

1/2 teaspoon minced garlic

1/8 teaspoon freshly
ground black pepper, or
to taste

Pinch cayenne pepper, or
to taste

Dash salt, or to taste

</td></tr>
</table>

This refreshing green purée adds a lively touch to green salads and is especially attractive when garnished with shredded carrots. Add a few strips of cold roast beef, a loaf of crusty bread, and you've got a quick and tasty meal.

Place all ingredients in a blender; purée until smooth. Taste; adjust seasonings. Stir or shake before serving.

ADVANCE PREPARATION: This dressing will keep for 4 days in a tightly closed container in the refrigerator.

PER TABLESPOON: CALORIES 77 • FAT 8.4G • CHOL 0 • SODIUM 2MG

Tip: Cayenne pepper, the ground dried pod of the small, more pungent varieties of chili peppers, should be used with restraint because it is very hot. Buy cayenne pepper in small quantities because the flavor and color will diminish over time; store it in a tightly closed container in the refrigerator.

GREEN PEPPERCORN VINAIGRETTE

MAKES 1/2 CUP

1/4 cup red wine vinegar

2 tablespoons hazelnut oil
(see page 6)

2 tablespoons extra-virgin
olive oil

1 teaspoon green pepper-
corns in brine (drained
and rinsed), or more to
taste (see tip)

1 teaspoon minced shallot

1/2 teaspoon Dijon
mustard

Dash salt, or to taste

*The pleasant pungency of green peppercorns adds a
particularly nice complement to fish and shellfish salads.*

Place all ingredients in a blender; blend until smooth.
Taste; adjust seasonings. Stir or shake before serving.

ADVANCE PREPARATION: This dressing will keep for 1 week in
a tightly closed container in the refrigerator.

PER TABLESPOON: CALORIES 60 • FAT 6.7G • CHOL 0 • SODIUM .9MG
(NUTRITIONAL DATA ON GREEN PEPPERCORNS ARE NOT AVAILABLE;
SODIUM MAY BE SLIGHTLY HIGHER.)

Tip: Green peppercorns are unripe pepper berries which,
instead of being dried, are preserved in brine; rinse them and
then crush or purée before using. They share the basic taste of
dried pepper and also have a sharp, almost acidic flavor.

HAZELNUT VINAIGRETTE

MAKES 1/2 CUP
1/4 cup red wine vinegar
3 tablespoons hazelnut oil (see page 6)
1 tablespoon extra-virgin olive oil
1 teaspoon Dijon mustard
1/8 teaspoon freshly ground black pepper, or to taste
Pinch salt, or to taste

Since hazelnut oil has a rather pronounced flavor, use this vinaigrette on a mixture of bitter and pungent greens, perhaps topped with thin apple slices and garnished with a few hazelnuts. Warmed, this mixture is memorable drizzled over grilled or uncooked pear slices artfully arranged with tender greens.

In a small bowl, whisk together all ingredients. Taste; adjust seasonings. Whisk or shake before serving.

ADVANCE PREPARATION: This dressing will keep for 1 week in a tightly closed container in the refrigerator.

PER TABLESPOON: CALORIES 60 • FAT 6.8G • CHOL 0 • SODIUM 2MG

HERBED ANCHOVY DRESSING

MAKES 1/2 CUP

1/4 cup white wine vinegar

3 tablespoons extra-virgin olive oil

1 tablespoon chopped anchovies (about 6 flat anchovy fillets)

2 teaspoons minced shallot

1 teaspoon Worcestershire sauce

1 teaspoon fresh thyme leaves (or 1/4 teaspoon dried thyme)

1 teaspoon minced fresh oregano (or 1/4 teaspoon dried oregano)

Dash freshly ground black pepper, or to taste

Here's an innovative, highly flavored combination to enliven pasta, vegetable, or seafood salads. I especially enjoy it drizzled over shrimp and garnished with capers.

Place all ingredients in a blender; purée until smooth. Taste; adjust seasonings. Whisk or shake before serving.

ADVANCE PREPARATION: If dried herbs are used, allow the dressing to stand for 15 to 30 minutes before serving. This dressing will keep for 2 days in a tightly closed container in the refrigerator.

PER TABLESPOON: CALORIES 53 • FAT 5.3G • CHOL 2MG • SODIUM 116MG

Tip: Anchovies are tiny, fatty fish with powerful flavor. They are cured by having most of the fat content removed by pressure and fermentation. Purchase them in tins filleted, brined, and preserved in oil.

HERBED TOMATO SAUCE

MAKES 1/2 CUP

2 tablespoons tomato paste

2 tablespoons extra-virgin
olive oil

2 tablespoons red wine
vinegar

2 tablespoons water

2 teaspoons minced fresh
basil (or 1/2 teaspoon
dried basil)

2 teaspoons minced fresh
oregano (or 1/2 teaspoon
dried oregano)

1/4 teaspoon minced garlic

1/4 teaspoon freshly
ground black pepper, or
to taste

For years, I have used this dressing on my favorite Pasta Primavera Salad: rotini tossed with steamed broccoli florets and cubed zucchini, chopped sweet red pepper, plum tomatoes, scallions, and peas. Generally, it is best to add the dressing to pasta salads no more than an hour in advance of serving because it tends to be absorbed into the noodles.

In a small bowl, whisk together all ingredients. Taste; adjust seasonings. Stir before serving.

ADVANCE PREPARATION: If dried herbs are used, allow the dressing to stand for 15 to 30 minutes before serving. It will keep for 1 week in a tightly closed container in the refrigerator. If fresh herbs are used, the dressing will keep for 4 days.

PER TABLESPOON: CALORIES 34 • FAT 3.4G • CHOL 0 • SODIUM 3MG

Tip: Oregano (wild marjoram) is an aromatic herb with a flavor similar to sweet marjoram, but stronger. Use it sparingly with tomatoes, potatoes, zucchini, eggplant, and all meats, poultry, and seafood.

HONEY-MINT DRESSING

MAKES 1/2 CUP
1/4 cup white rice vinegar
2 tablespoons safflower oil
3 tablespoons honey
2 teaspoons minced fresh mint (or 1/2 teaspoon dried mint)
1/8 teaspoon freshly ground black pepper, or to taste

There's nothing quite like the cool and refreshing taste of mint on a scorching summer day. My favorite summer salad is made with this dressing served on romaine lettuce topped with halved fresh strawberries, halved grapes, and toasted slivered almonds.

In a small bowl, whisk together all ingredients. Taste; adjust seasonings. Whisk or shake before serving.

ADVANCE PREPARATION: If dried mint is used, allow the dressing to stand for 15 to 30 minutes before serving; it will keep for 1 week in a tightly closed container in the refrigerator. If fresh mint is used, the dressing will keep for 4 days.

PER TABLESPOON: CALORIES 55 • FAT 3.4G • CHOL 0 • SODIUM .6MG

Tip: Mint, providing an aromatic, sweet, and refreshing flavor with a cool aftertaste, is an ideal complement to hot, spicy foods. Of the many varieties, spearmint is the most common. An easy-to-grow perennial, fresh mint is far more acceptable than dried.

HONEY–POPPY SEED DRESSING

MAKES 1/2 CUP
1/4 cup white rice vinegar
2 tablespoons safflower oil
3 tablespoons honey
1/2 teaspoon poppy seeds
1/8 teaspoon freshly ground black pepper, or to taste

his dressing has proved so popular that it's become a household staple. I nearly always have a container of this dressing ready in my refrigerator. It is equally as delicious drizzled over greens or a bowl of fresh fruit—or try the two in tasty combination!

In a small bowl, whisk together all ingredients. Taste; adjust seasonings. Whisk or shake before serving.

ADVANCE PREPARATION: This dressing will keep for 1 week in a tightly closed container in the refrigerator.

PER TABLESPOON: CALORIES 56 • FAT 3.5G • CHOL 0 • SODIUM .5MG

Tip: Poppy seeds will add texture and a distinctively pleasant, walnutlike flavor to your dressings.

HOT PEPPER VINAIGRETTE

MAKES 1/2 CUP

1/4 cup red wine vinegar

2 tablespoons safflower oil

2 teaspoons hot pepper oil,
or to taste

1 teaspoon toasted sesame
seeds (see page 41)

1 teaspoon honey

1/2 teaspoon minced garlic

1/2 teaspoon minced fresh
gingerroot, or to taste

This dressing is guaranteed to awaken your taste buds. For tips on hot pepper oil, see page 7—and remember that Chinese hot pepper oil is much more intense than Italian pepper oil. Either can be used in this recipe.

In a small bowl, whisk together all ingredients. Taste; adjust seasonings. Stir or shake before serving.

ADVANCE PREPARATION: This dressing will keep for 1 week in a tightly closed container in the refrigerator.

PER TABLESPOON: CALORIES **45** • FAT **4.7G** • CHOL **0** • SODIUM **.2MG**

Tip: Powdered dry ginger is a poor substitute for the fresh root and will not duplicate the distinctive ginger flavor. My favorite method for keeping fresh gingerroot on hand is to wrap the entire root in an airtight foil wrap and freeze. Without thawing, use a fine grater to grate off the amount needed. Rewrap the remainder of the gingerroot and replace it immediately in the freezer; it will remain flavorful for 3 months. Minced fresh gingerroot is also available in the produce department of most supermarkets; this form is also acceptable.

ITALIAN DRESSING

MAKES 1/2 CUP

1/4 cup white wine vinegar

1/4 cup extra-virgin olive oil

1 teaspoon minced shallot

1 teaspoon minced fresh parsley

1 teaspoon minced fresh chives (do not substitute dried chives; if fresh are not available, substitute julienned scallion greens)

1 teaspoon minced fresh oregano (or 1/4 teaspoon dried oregano)

Pinch crushed red pepper, or to taste

Pinch dry mustard powder, or to taste

Dash white pepper, or to taste

Be sure to try this aromatic dressing. It will add a flourish to any salad greens, especially when topped with Herbed Garlic Croutons (page 139), which will make your salad even more scrumptious!

In a small bowl, whisk together all ingredients. Taste; adjust seasonings. Whisk or shake before serving.

ADVANCE PREPARATION: If dried oregano is used, allow the dressing to stand for 15 to 30 minutes before serving; it will keep for 1 week in a tightly closed container in the refrigerator. If fresh oregano is used, the dressing will keep for 4 days.

PER TABLESPOON: CALORIES 61 • FAT 6.7G • CHOL 0 • SODIUM .2MG

LEMON-BASIL VINAIGRETTE

MAKES 1/2 CUP

1/4 cup extra-virgin olive oil

1/2 teaspoon lemon zest (see tip)

1/4 cup freshly squeezed lemon juice

1 tablespoon minced fresh basil (do not use dried basil)

1/4 teaspoon cracked peppercorns, or to taste (see page 94)

Pinch sugar, or to taste

Dash salt, or to taste

Try it once, and you'll wonder how you ever lived without it! Fragrant with the pungent aromas of fresh lemon juice, fresh basil, olive oil, and cracked peppercorns, this dressing is destined to become a favorite for all your summer vegetable salads.

In a small bowl, whisk together all ingredients. Taste; adjust seasonings. Whisk or shake before serving.

ADVANCE PREPARATION: This dressing will keep for 2 days in a tightly closed container in the refrigerator.

PER TABLESPOON: CALORIES **62** • FAT **6.7G** • CHOL **0** • SODIUM **.3MG**

Tip: Zesting is done with a kitchen gadget called a zester, which has a short, flat blade with a beveled end and 5 small holes. When drawn firmly over the skin of a lemon, lime, or orange, the tool removes long, thin strips of the colored zest (see page 18).

LEMON-CINNAMON VINAIGRETTE

MAKES 1/2 CUP

1/3 cup freshly squeezed lemon juice

3 tablespoons extra-virgin olive oil

1/2 teaspoon ground cinnamon

1/2 teaspoon freshly ground black pepper

1/4 teaspoon turmeric

Few drops hot pepper sauce, or to taste

I originally developed this dressing for a mixture of couscous or rice, toasted pine nuts, celery, scallions, parsley, and currants. The combination of lemon and cinnamon lends just the right Middle Eastern note.

In a small bowl, whisk together all ingredients. Taste; adjust seasonings. Whisk or shake before serving.

ADVANCE PREPARATION: This dressing will keep for 2 days in a tightly closed container in the refrigerator.

PER TABLESPOON: CALORIES 48 • FAT 5.1G • CHOL 0 • SODIUM .2MG

Tip: Once opened, refrigerate the bottle of hot pepper sauce to retain the flavor and color.

MAPLE-CRANBERRY VINAIGRETTE

MAKES 1/2 CUP
1/4 cup safflower oil
3 tablespoons cranberry juice
1 tablespoon maple syrup

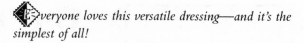*veryone loves this versatile dressing—and it's the simplest of all!*

In a small bowl, whisk together all ingredients. Whisk or shake before serving.

ADVANCE PREPARATION: This dressing will keep for 2 days in a tightly closed container in the refrigerator.

PER TABLESPOON: CALORIES 64 • FAT 6.8G • CHOL 0 • SODIUM .2MG

MARMALADE VINAIGRETTE

MAKES 1/2 CUP

- 3 tablespoons freshly squeezed orange juice
- 2 tablespoons safflower oil
- 2 tablespoons orange marmalade
- 1 tablespoon Dijon mustard
- 1/2 teaspoon curry powder, or to taste
- Dash freshly ground black pepper, or to taste

Orange marmalade and Dijon mustard at first may seem like an unlikely combination, but trust me, the mixture is delicious—especially on chicken and wild rice.

In a small bowl, whisk together all ingredients. Taste; adjust seasonings. Whisk or shake before serving.

ADVANCE PREPARATION: This dressing will keep for 2 days in a tightly closed container in the refrigerator.

PER TABLESPOON: CALORIES 47 • FAT 3.4G • CHOL 0 • SODIUM 5MG

MESQUITE TOMATO DRESSING

MAKES 1/2 CUP

3 tablespoons ketchup

3 tablespoons safflower oil

2 tablespoons red wine
vinegar

1 tablespoon water

1/2 teaspoon sugar

2 teaspoons minced fresh
oregano (or 1/2 teaspoon
dried oregano)

1/2 teaspoon
Worcestershire sauce

1/4 teaspoon mesquite
liquid smoke, or to taste

1/8 teaspoon freshly
ground black pepper, or
to taste

Dash salt, or to taste

The touch of mesquite provides a barbecue flavor that goes especially well with strips of broiled chicken, beef, or fish; it also turns legumes into an interesting side salad.

In a small bowl, whisk together all ingredients. Taste; adjust seasonings. Whisk or shake before serving.

ADVANCE PREPARATION: If dried oregano is used, allow the dressing to stand for 15 to 30 minutes before serving; it will keep for 1 week in a tightly closed container in the refrigerator. If fresh oregano is used, the dressing will keep for 4 days.

PER TABLESPOON: CALORIES 52 • FAT 5.1G • CHOL 0 • SODIUM 62MG

ORANGE VINAIGRETTE

MAKES 1/2 CUP

1/3 cup white rice vinegar

2 tablespoons frozen orange juice concentrate (undiluted), thawed

1/2 teaspoon dry mustard powder

1/4 teaspoon minced garlic

1/4 teaspoon celery seeds

Dash white pepper, or to taste

For a light, low-fat salad, toss this tangy vinaigrette with greens, orange segments, and strips of red onion. It also adds a zesty touch to fruit salads.

In a small bowl, whisk together all ingredients. Taste; adjust seasonings. Whisk or shake before serving.

ADVANCE PREPARATION: This dressing will keep for 2 days in a tightly closed container in the refrigerator.

PER TABLESPOON: CALORIES 7 • FAT .02G • CHOL 0 • SODIUM .3MG

Tip: Celery seeds are the tiny, aromatic seeds of the celery plant. Use them when the taste rather than the texture of celery is desired. They provide good flavoring for cabbage, cauliflower, fish, fruit, potato, and tomato salads.

PAPAYA–POPPY SEED VINAIGRETTE

MAKES 1/2 CUP
1 cup 1/2-inch papaya cubes
1/4 cup freshly squeezed lime juice
1 tablespoon safflower oil
1 tablespoon honey, or to taste
1/2 teaspoon poppy seeds

If you're passionate about papayas, you'll love this tropically inspired dressing. For a delicious and colorful salad, pair it with shrimp or scallops; garnish with a wedge of lime.

Place all ingredients, except poppy seeds, in a blender; blend until smooth. Stir in poppy seeds. Chill. Stir before serving.

ADVANCE PREPARATION: This dressing will keep for a day in a tightly closed container in the refrigerator.

PER TABLESPOON: CALORIES 33 • FAT 1.8G • CHOL 0 • SODIUM .8MG

Tip: Papayas are ripe when the skin is a deep yellow or orange and the flesh is slightly soft to pressure. Slightly unripe papayas can be ripened by storing them in a pierced paper bag at room temperature for a few days.

PAPRIKA VINAIGRETTE

MAKES 1/2 CUP

1/4 cup safflower oil

1/4 cup white wine vinegar

2 teaspoons honey

1/2 teaspoon paprika

Pinch cayenne pepper, or
  to taste

like the lively flavors of this dressing so much that I invented a special salad to set them off. It's a toss of Belgian endive, cubed apple, grated carrots, pecans, and currants. The result: a delicious combination of bitter, sweet, and spicy elements.

In a small bowl, whisk together all ingredients. Taste; adjust seasonings. Whisk or shake before serving.

ADVANCE PREPARATION: This dressing will keep for 1 week in a tightly closed container in the refrigerator.

PER TABLESPOON: CALORIES 67 • FAT 6.8G • CHOL 0 • SODIUM .2MG

Tip: Paprika is a bright red powder made from a certain variety of pepper. The most flavorful variety comes from Hungary, where its pungency ranges from mild to very hot. Store it in the refrigerator to preserve color and flavor.

PARMESAN VINAIGRETTE

1/4 cup extra-virgin olive oil

2 tablespoons red wine vinegar

2 tablespoons freshly squeezed lemon juice

2 tablespoons freshly grated Parmesan cheese

1 teaspoon Dijon mustard

1/2 teaspoon minced garlic

1 teaspoon minced fresh oregano (or 1/4 teaspoon dried oregano)

1/4 teaspoon freshly ground black pepper, or to taste

Dash salt, or to taste

This dressing seems right at home on a bed of greens topped with tomatoes, but it is also ideal for bringing out the flavors of a pasta salad.

In a small bowl, whisk together all ingredients. Taste; adjust seasonings. Whisk or shake before serving.

ADVANCE PREPARATION: If dried oregano is used, allow the dressing to stand for 15 to 30 minutes before serving. This dressing will keep for 2 days in a tightly closed container in the refrigerator.

PER TABLESPOON: CALORIES 68 • FAT 7.2G • CHOL 1MG • SODIUM 31MG

Tip: Parmesan cheese should always be grated fresh for the best flavor, rather than purchased in the pregrated form, which is usually loaded with preservatives. Kept in a tightly closed container, freshly grated Parmesan will keep in the refrigerator for about a week. If you buy a block of Parmesan, keep it tightly wrapped in plastic wrap; wrapped properly, it will keep for 2 to 4 weeks.

PESTO VINAIGRETTE

MAKES 1/2 CUP
3 tablespoons red wine vinegar
2 tablespoons extra-virgin olive oil
2 tablespoons Basil Pesto (page 138)
1 tablespoon freshly squeezed lemon juice
1 teaspoon Dijon mustard
1/4 teaspoon freshly ground black pepper, or to taste
Dash salt, or to taste

If you love pesto—and who doesn't?—you'll love the character it adds to this vinaigrette. It's hard to beat the heady aroma of fresh basil!

In a small bowl, whisk together all ingredients. Taste; adjust seasonings. Whisk or shake before serving.

ADVANCE PREPARATION: This dressing will keep for 2 days in a tightly closed container in the refrigerator.

PER TABLESPOON: CALORIES 50 • FAT 5.4G • CHOL 0 • SODIUM 3MG

VARIATION:
• add freshly grated Parmesan cheese

PINEAPPLE-SESAME VINAIGRETTE

MAKES 1/2 CUP

1/4 cup frozen pineapple
juice concentrate
(undiluted), thawed

3 tablespoons white rice
vinegar

1 tablespoon water

1 teaspoon dark sesame oil
(see page 6)

1 teaspoon low-sodium soy
sauce

1/2 teaspoon minced fresh
gingerroot, or to taste

1/4 teaspoon minced garlic

---

ruity and with a hint of sesame oil, this dressing is delightfully light and versatile. Try it on mild-flavored greens tossed with mandarin oranges and garnished with toasted almond slices.

In a small bowl, whisk together all ingredients. Whisk or shake before serving.

ADVANCE PREPARATION: This dressing will keep for 2 days in a tightly closed container in the refrigerator.

PER TABLESPOON: CALORIES 10 • FAT .6G • CHOL 0 • SODIUM 23MG

PISTACHIO VINAIGRETTE

MAKES 1/2 CUP

1/4 cup mirin or aji-mirin
(sweetened rice wine—
see page 9)

3 tablespoons pistachio oil
(see page 6)

1 tablespoon safflower oil

1 tablespoon water

1 teaspoon minced shallot

1 teaspoon fresh thyme
leaves (or 1/4 teaspoon
dried thyme)

1/2 teaspoon minced garlic

Dash freshly ground black
pepper, or to taste

Although pistachio oil is not always available in supermarkets, it is worth a trip to a specialty market if you like the distinctive flavor of this "gourmet" nut. And the sweet flavor of mirin is the perfect flavor complement. Serve this elegant dressing on a variety of greens such as Bibb, radicchio, and watercress, topped with a nutty-flavored cheese such as Asiago; and, of course, a sprinkling of pistachio nuts is essential!

In a small bowl, whisk together all ingredients. Taste; adjust seasonings. Whisk or shake before serving.

ADVANCE PREPARATION: If dried thyme is used, allow the dressing to stand for 15 to 30 minutes before serving; it will keep for 1 week in a tightly closed container in the refrigerator. If fresh thyme is used, the dressing will keep for 4 days.

PER TABLESPOON: CALORIES 66 • FAT 6.8G • CHOL 0 • SODIUM .6MG

Tip: When using fresh thyme, it is not necessary to remove the tiny leaves one by one. Hold the sprig in one hand, and with the other, scrape downward with your fingers, removing most of the leaves. The leaves can be used without mincing; the tender stems at the tip can be minced.

RASPBERRY-WALNUT VINAIGRETTE

MAKES 1/2 CUP

1/4 cup raspberry vinegar

3 tablespoons walnut oil
(see page 6)

1 tablespoon freshly
squeezed lemon juice

1/2 teaspoon Dijon
mustard

1 tablespoon minced fresh
parsley

Dash freshly ground black
pepper, or to taste

I like this dressing both chilled and warm. Try it drizzled over sliced fresh pears arranged on a bed of romaine lettuce; garnish with chopped walnuts. It's delicious on chicken, too!

In a small bowl, whisk together all ingredients. Taste; adjust seasonings. Whisk or shake before serving.

ADVANCE PREPARATION: This dressing will keep for 2 days in a tightly closed container in the refrigerator.

PER TABLESPOON: CALORIES 45 • FAT 5.1G • CHOL 0 • SODIUM 1MG

Tip: To mince fresh parsley very finely, place it under running water to clean, then dry it with a dish towel so the pieces will not stick together as you mince it.

ROASTED GARLIC VINAIGRETTE

MAKES 1/2 CUP
1 whole garlic bulb
1/4 cup plus about 1/4 teaspoon extra-virgin olive oil
2 tablespoons balsamic vinegar
1 tablespoon white wine vinegar
1 tablespoon water
1/2 teaspoon honey, or to taste
1/8 teaspoon freshly ground black pepper, or to taste
Dash salt, or to taste

asting is believing: It may seem outlandish to use 10 cloves of garlic in this dressing, but roasting garlic gives it a rich, sweet flavor without the harshness of raw garlic.

Preheat oven to 400°F. Line a baking sheet or small pan with aluminum foil.

To prepare the garlic bulb for roasting, remove the loose, excess papery skin, but leave the cloves intact. Trim off the top stem. Brush the outer skin and top with about 1/4 teaspoon olive oil. Place on the prepared baking sheet or pan. Bake for about 10 minutes, until the cloves feel soft when pressed. Remove from the baking sheet or pan and allow the bulb to cool.

Separate 10 individual garlic cloves. Slice away the bottom from each and squeeze out the flesh. Place in a blender with the remaining ingredients. Purée until smooth. Taste; adjust seasonings. Stir before serving.

ADVANCE PREPARATION: This dressing will keep for 2 days in a tightly closed container in the refrigerator. After standing, it thickens; thin by stirring in water.

PER TABLESPOON: CALORIES 70 • FAT 6.7G • CHOL 0 • SODIUM 1MG

Tip: Leftover roasted garlic cloves are delicious as a spread for French bread. Whole or chopped, they can be used as an ingredient in other recipes calling for garlic.

ROASTED SWEET RED PEPPER DRESSING

MAKES 1/2 CUP

1 medium-size red bell pepper

1 tablespoon red wine vinegar

1 tablespoon garlic-infused extra-virgin olive oil

1/4 teaspoon freshly ground black pepper, or to taste

Dash salt, or to taste

Because I love the sweet, pure flavor of roasted red bell peppers, I usually do not add herbs to this dressing. But occasionally, for variety, after puréeing, I stir in basil, rosemary, or mint. This dressing is versatile; I use it most often on mild-flavored fish, chicken, or a potato salad garnished with capers. And warm, it's especially delicious drizzled over thin, diagonally cut strips of grilled or broiled chicken.

Adjust oven rack about 3 inches from the heating element; preheat the broiler.

Remove the stem and cut the bell pepper in half lengthwise; discard the seeds and membranes. Place the pepper, skin side up, on a foil-lined baking sheet; flatten with the palm of your hand. Broil for 5 to 8 minutes or until the skins are blackened, charred, and blistered.

Place the pepper in a zip-top, heavy-duty plastic bag and seal; let stand for 10 to 15 minutes (the steam will loosen the skins). Peel and discard the skins; cut into 1-inch pieces.

Put the pepper in a blender along with the remaining ingredients. Purée the mixture to obtain a smooth sauce. Taste; adjust seasonings. Chill. Stir before serving.

ADVANCE PREPARATION: This dressing will keep for 2 days in a tightly closed container in the refrigerator.

PER TABLESPOON: CALORIES 18 • FAT 1.7G • CHOL 0 • SODIUM .2MG

SAVORY VINAIGRETTE

Makes 1/2 cup
1/4 cup white wine vinegar
1/4 cup extra-virgin olive oil
1 tablespoon minced fresh summer savory (or 1 teaspoon dried summer savory)
1 tablespoon coarsely chopped fresh parsley
1/2 teaspoon minced garlic
1/4 teaspoon dry mustard powder
1/8 teaspoon freshly ground black pepper, or to taste
Pinch salt, or to taste

Parisian charcuteries (delis) have been the source of inspiration for several of my favorite out-of-the-ordinary salads. Try this vinaigrette tossed with unpeeled new potatoes and yams or sweet potatoes, chopped shallot, and perhaps chunks of chicken—a potato salad quite different from the one Mom used to make!

In a small bowl, whisk together all ingredients. Taste; adjust seasonings. Whisk or shake before serving.

ADVANCE PREPARATION: If dried summer savory is used, allow the dressing to stand for 15 to 30 minutes before serving; it will keep for 1 week in a tightly closed container in the refrigerator. If fresh summer savory is used, the dressing will keep for 4 days.

PER TABLESPOON: CALORIES 61 • FAT 6.8G • CHOL 0 • SODIUM .7MG

Tip: Summer savory, similar to thyme but more delicate, is a very versatile, slightly peppery herb. It is excellent with beans, fish, lamb, pork, poultry, potatoes, tomatoes, and tossed greens.

SESAME-ORANGE DRESSING

MAKES 1/2 CUP

1/2 teaspoon grated orange rind

1/3 cup freshly squeezed orange juice

1 tablespoon sugar

1 tablespoon safflower oil

1 teaspoon white rice vinegar

1 teaspoon dark sesame oil (see page 6)

1 teaspoon low-sodium soy sauce

1/2 teaspoon toasted sesame seeds (see page 41)

The magic of this recipe is in the blending of the flavors. Use it to complement mild-flavored fish and vegetables— or to create a unique coleslaw!

In a small bowl, whisk together all ingredients, making certain the sugar is dissolved. Whisk or shake before serving.

ADVANCE PREPARATION: This dressing will keep for 2 days in a tightly closed container in the refrigerator.

PER TABLESPOON: CALORIES 32 • FAT 2.4G • CHOL 0 • SODIUM 23MG

SESAME-SOY DRESSING

MAKES 1/2 CUP

1/3 cup white rice vinegar

2 tablespoons low-sodium soy sauce

1 teaspoon dark sesame oil (see page 6)

1 teaspoon minced fresh gingerroot, or to taste (see page 52)

1 teaspoon sugar

1/2 teaspoon minced garlic

1/2 teaspoon toasted sesame seeds (see page 41)

Dash white pepper, or to taste

This dressing is the perfect topping for salads to accompany your menus with an oriental theme. If you want to add a little heat, add 1/4 teaspoon Chinese hot oil or a pinch of crushed red pepper.

In a small bowl, whisk together all ingredients, making certain the sugar is dissolved. Taste; adjust seasonings. Whisk or shake before serving.

ADVANCE PREPARATION: This dressing will keep for 1 week in a tightly closed container in the refrigerator.

PER TABLESPOON: CALORIES 11 • FAT .7G • CHOL 0 • SODIUM 139MG

Tip: Low-sodium or "lite" soy sauce contains less sodium than traditional soy sauce or tamari, but can be used in the same proportions since it provides nearly the same flavor.

SHALLOT AND CAPER DRESSING

MAKES 1/2 CUP
1/4 cup red wine vinegar
1/4 cup extra-virgin olive oil
1 tablespoon minced shallot
2 teaspoons capers, drained
Dash freshly ground black pepper, or to taste
Dash salt, or to taste

This dressing will turn that "Not again!" canned tuna into something special, especially with the addition of tomatoes, olives, and a garnish of feta cheese.

In a small bowl, whisk together all ingredients. Taste; adjust seasonings. Whisk or shake before serving.

ADVANCE PREPARATION: The flavor of this dressing improves after setting overnight or longer. It will keep for 1 week in a tightly closed container in the refrigerator.

PER TABLESPOON: CALORIES 61 • FAT 6.8G • CHOL 0 • SODIUM 14MG

Tip: Capers are the unopened flower buds of a Mediterranean shrub. Size varies; the largest have the strongest flavor; the smallest, "nonpareil," are the most subtle in flavor, the most tender, and the most expensive. Once opened, store in the refrigerator for no more than 2 to 3 months.

SOUTHWESTERN DRIED CHILI PEPPER DRESSING

MAKES 1/2 CUP

1 medium-size dried Anaheim chili pepper

1 cup boiling water

3 tablespoons extra-virgin olive oil

2 tablespoons freshly squeezed lime juice (or red wine vinegar)

1 tablespoon minced onion

1 tablespoon tomato paste (see page 99)

1 teaspoon light brown sugar

1/2 teaspoon minced garlic

1/8 teaspoon freshly ground black pepper, or to taste

Dash salt, or to taste

Pinch ground cumin

1 tablespoon coarsely chopped fresh cilantro, or to taste (do not substitute dried coriander)

Pinch crushed red pepper, optional

Enjoy this dressing on greens and broiled, chilled fish or chicken. Your favorite dried chilies can be substituted for the dried Anaheim chili pepper.

Rinse the dried Anaheim pepper; remove the stem and seeds. Place in a small bowl and add the boiling water. Allow to stand for at least 15 minutes.

When the pepper has softened, coarsely chop (it should equal about 3 tablespoons) and place in a blender along with 3 tablespoons of the soaking liquid. Add the remaining ingredients, except the fresh cilantro and crushed red pepper. Purée the mixture until smooth. Stir through a mesh strainer to remove the bits of peel. Stir in the cilantro. Taste; adjust seasonings. Add the crushed red pepper if you want a hotter flavor.

If possible, allow the dressing to stand at room temperature for a half hour before using to allow the flavors to blend. Stir before serving.

ADVANCE PREPARATION: This dressing will keep for 2 days in a tightly closed container in the refrigerator.

PER TABLESPOON: CALORIES 51 • FAT 5.1G • CHOL 0 • SODIUM 2MG

Tip: Store dried chili peppers in an airtight container at room temperature for up to 4 months, or longer in the refrigerator.

SUMMER PEACH VINAIGRETTE

MAKES 1/2 CUP
1 medium-size peach, peeled, seeded, and sliced
2 tablespoons safflower oil
1 tablespoon freshly squeezed lemon juice
1 tablespoon rice vinegar
1 teaspoon honey, or to taste
Dash freshly ground black pepper, or to taste

On a hot summer evening, capture the pleasures of the season by serving this sweet and fruity vinaigrette over greens or fruit—perhaps with the addition of a piece of chilled broiled or grilled fish.

Place all ingredients in a blender; purée until smooth. Taste; adjust seasonings. Chill. Stir before serving.

ADVANCE PREPARATION: This dressing will keep for 1 day in a tightly closed container in the refrigerator.

PER TABLESPOON: CALORIES 38 • FAT 3.4G • CHOL 0 • SODIUM .1MG

SUN-DRIED TOMATO–ROSEMARY VINAIGRETTE

MAKES 1/2 CUP

4 sun-dried tomatoes (marinated in olive oil), minced

1/4 cup extra-virgin olive oil

3 tablespoons freshly squeezed lemon juice

1 teaspoon Dijon mustard

2 teaspoons minced fresh rosemary (or 1/4 teaspoon dried rosemary, crushed)

1/8 teaspoon freshly ground black pepper, or to taste

Dash salt, or to taste

ere's a good choice for a busy day when you want to perk up a quickly prepared salad. I think you'll enjoy the rich, sweet flavor of the sun-dried tomatoes. Allow standing time if dried rosemary is used.

In a small bowl, whisk together all ingredients. Taste; adjust seasonings. Whisk or shake before serving.

ADVANCE PREPARATION: To improve the texture and enhance the flavor, crush dried rosemary leaves between your fingers, mash them with a mortar and pestle, or chop them thoroughly before adding to your recipe. If used fresh, the leaves should be minced. If dried rosemary is used, allow the dressing to stand for a few hours before serving. The dressing will keep for 2 days in a tightly closed container in the refrigerator.

PER TABLESPOON: CALORIES 76 • FAT 6.8G • CHOL 0 • SODIUM 8MG

VARIATION:
- omit the rosemary; for the extra-virgin olive oil, substitute rosemary-infused extra-virgin olive oil

Tip: If not marinated, sun-dried tomatoes must be hydrated before using. Pour boiling water over them and allow to stand for 15 to 20 minutes, then drain. They can be used immediately or marinated in olive oil for later use.

SWEET AND SOUR DRESSING

MAKES 1/2 CUP

1/4 cup white rice vinegar

1/4 cup safflower oil

1 tablespoon light brown sugar

1 tablespoon sugar

1 tablespoon minced shallot

1/2 teaspoon dry mustard powder

Pinch crushed red pepper, or to taste

Dash white pepper, or to taste

Dash salt, or to taste

Serve on a spinach and mushroom salad or over thin slices of cucumber. These flavors make a great accompaniment to oriental stir-fried entrées.

In a small bowl, stir together all ingredients, making certain the sugars are dissolved. Whisk or shake before serving.

ADVANCE PREPARATION: This dressing will keep for 2 days in a tightly closed container in the refrigerator.

PER TABLESPOON: CALORIES **74** • FAT **6.8G** • CHOL **0** • SODIUM **.7MG**

Tip: Shallots provide a blend of onion and garlic flavors. For 1 tablespoon of minced fresh shallot, you can substitute 1 tablespoon minced onion and 1/2 teaspoon minced garlic.

TARRAGON VINAIGRETTE

MAKES 1/2 CUP

1/4 cup tarragon white
wine vinegar

1/4 cup safflower oil

1/2 teaspoon sugar

1 tablespoon minced fresh
tarragon (or 1/2 teaspoon
dried tarragon)

1/2 teaspoon minced garlic

1/4 teaspoon Dijon
mustard

1/8 teaspoon freshly
ground black pepper, or
to taste

Pinch crushed red pepper,
or to taste

Dash salt, or to taste

ry this elegant dressing on greens topped with sliced mushrooms or chunks of chicken. The flavors of these foods are particularly compatible with tarragon.

In a small bowl, whisk together all ingredients, making certain the sugar is dissolved. Taste; adjust seasonings. Whisk or shake before serving.

ADVANCE PREPARATION: If dried tarragon is used, allow the dressing to stand for 15 to 30 minutes before serving; it will keep for 1 week in a tightly closed container in the refrigerator. If fresh tarragon is used, the dressing will keep for 4 days.

PER TABLESPOON: CALORIES 63 • FAT 6.8G • CHOL 0 • SODIUM .6MG

THAI GINGER-LIME DRESSING

<table>
<tr><td colspan="2">MAKES 1/2 CUP</td></tr>
</table>

MAKES 1/2 CUP

1/4 cup freshly squeezed
  lime juice

1/4 cup unsalted,
  dry-roasted peanuts

1 piece peeled fresh
  gingerroot (1 inch by
  2 inches), cut into 1/8-
  inch slices

1/2 jalapeño pepper, seeds
  removed

2 tablespoons low-sodium
  soy sauce

1 tablespoon safflower oil

1 tablespoon sugar

2 tablespoons minced fresh
  basil (do not substitute
  dried basil)

This delightfully spicy mixture is the perfect dressing to counteract the doldrums of bland food. I like to toss it with cellophane noodles; it is also delicious with a combination of buckwheat noodles, cucumbers, and shrimp.

Place all ingredients, except basil, in a blender; purée until smooth. Stir in basil. Whisk or shake before serving.

ADVANCE PREPARATION: This dressing will keep for 2 days in a tightly closed container in the refrigerator.

PER TABLESPOON: CALORIES 53 • FAT 4G • CHOL 0 • SODIUM 133MG

VARIATIONS:
- for the lime juice, substitute lemon juice
- for a hotter flavor, substitute red, hot chili pepper for the jalapeño pepper
- for the basil, substitute fresh cilantro or mint

VEGETABLE JUICE VINAIGRETTE

MAKES 1/2 CUP

1/4 cup mixed-vegetable juice or tomato juice

2 tablespoons garlic-infused extra-virgin olive oil (or 2 tablespoons extra-virgin olive oil plus a dash of minced garlic, to taste)

2 tablespoons red wine vinegar

1 teaspoon freshly squeezed lemon juice

1/2 teaspoon Dijon mustard

1 teaspoon minced fresh basil (or 1/4 teaspoon dried basil)

1 teaspoon minced fresh oregano (or 1/4 teaspoon dried oregano)

1/8 teaspoon freshly ground black pepper, or to taste

call this my "emergency" dressing. Using canned vegetable juice (or tomato juice) and dried herbs, this dressing can be made quickly using ingredients usually on hand. Toss it with chilled pasta and steamed vegetables for a low-fat lunch entrée for unexpected guests.

In a small bowl, whisk together all ingredients. Taste; adjust seasonings. Whisk or shake before serving.

ADVANCE PREPARATION: If dried herbs are used, allow the dressing to stand for 15 to 30 minutes before serving; it will keep for 1 week in a tightly closed container in the refrigerator. If fresh herbs are used, the dressing will keep for 4 days.

PER TABLESPOON: CALORIES 32 • FAT 3.4G • CHOL 0 • SODIUM 27MG

ZESTY LEMON-LIME VINAIGRETTE

MAKES 1/2 CUP

1/4 cup safflower oil

2 tablespoons freshly
squeezed lime juice

2 tablespoons freshly
squeezed lemon juice

1/4 teaspoon minced garlic

1/4 teaspoon ground
cumin

1/4 teaspoon chili powder

1/8 teaspoon freshly
ground black pepper, or
to taste

Pinch cayenne pepper, or
to taste

Dash salt, or to taste

There is nothing subtle about the gutsy flavors in this dressing, which is at its best tossed with beans, chopped red bell pepper, cubes of tomato, and chopped red onion.

In a small bowl, whisk together all ingredients. Taste; adjust seasonings. Whisk or shake before serving.

ADVANCE PREPARATION: This dressing will keep for 2 days in a tightly closed container in the refrigerator.

PER TABLESPOON: CALORIES 63 • FAT 6.8G • CHOL 0 • SODIUM 2MG

Tip: Cumin has a warm, aromatic taste and is widely used in Spanish, Mexican, and Indian cooking. It is available in two forms: whole cumin and ground cumin seed, which is appropriate for salad dressings.

CREAMY DRESSINGS

FOR YEARS YOU may have been buying (and yawning over) the same old Ranch and Thousand Island dressings. But when it comes to creamy dressings, there are far more interesting possibilities. Creamy dressings can play many roles. They can be rich or light, sweet or tart. Among these recipes, you'll find a wide variety of fascinating flavors, from herbs and juice concentrates to peanut butter or anchovies. Here's your chance to experiment with some new tastes and textures.

Many of these versatile salad dressings are thick and full-bodied enough to be used also as vegetable or fruit dips. Many are equally as flavorful on fish, shellfish, or chicken as they are on greens and vegetables (see the helpful charts on pages 143–49).

While there are differences in taste and texture, for the sake of convenience and cutting fat and cholesterol, some of the creamy ingredients can be used interchangeably in these recipes. Yogurt, especially extra-thick plain yogurt, can usually be substituted for all or part of the mayonnaise or sour cream. Buttermilk also can be substituted, but the end result will be thinner in texture. In addition to fat and cholesterol content, the substitutions may also vary in sodium. For more information, see "Ingredients for Smooth, Creamy Texture" on pages 12–14.

Because dairy products are the base for creamy dressings, always start with very fresh ingredients; the dressings will then remain at their peak of flavor for about two days. Some improve in flavor if allowed to stand for a while before using. And some may thicken after standing and need to be thinned with milk or water before using. I prefer to use these dressings chilled.

Students in my cooking classes have been requesting a low-fat Caesar dressing. It's here! And so are Ranch and Thousand Island, at their best when made from scratch.

APPLE–CELERY SEED DRESSING

MAKES 1/2 CUP
1/3 cup low-fat plain yogurt
2 tablespoons frozen apple juice concentrate (undiluted), thawed
1 teaspoon honey
1/4 teaspoon celery seeds
Dash freshly ground black pepper, or to taste

This low calorie, fat-free dressing is excellent tossed with a mixture of shredded carrots, raisins, and sunflower seeds; or try it on mixed fruit.

In a small bowl, whisk together all ingredients. Taste; adjust seasonings. Stir before serving.

ADVANCE PREPARATION: This dressing will keep for 2 days in a tightly closed container in the refrigerator.

PER TABLESPOON: CALORIES 16 • FAT .2G • CHOL .6MG • SODIUM 8MG

APRICOT-YOGURT DRESSING

<table>
<tr><td>

MAKES **1/2** CUP

1/4 cup low-fat plain yogurt

2 tablespoons coarsely chopped dried apricots (about 3 apricots)

1 tablespoon safflower oil

1 tablespoon white rice vinegar

1 teaspoon honey

1/2 teaspoon minced onion

1/4 teaspoon celery seed

Dash dry mustard powder

Dash freshly ground black pepper, or to taste

</td></tr>
</table>

like to use this dressing to top a salad of romaine lettuce, spinach, avocado slices, bean sprouts, and toasted sliced almonds. It also can be used to create an interesting chicken salad.

Place yogurt, apricots, oil, vinegar, honey, and onion in a blender; purée until smooth. Stir in the celery seed, mustard powder, and pepper. Taste; adjust seasonings. Chill. Stir before serving.

ADVANCE PREPARATION: This dressing will keep for 2 days in a tightly closed container in the refrigerator. After standing, it thickens; thin by stirring in water.

PER TABLESPOON: CALORIES **28** • FAT **1.8**G • CHOL **.4**MG • SODIUM **5**MG

Tip: Dried fruits will keep for at least a year, especially if refrigerated in a tightly closed container. If they harden during storage, hydrate the dried fruits by soaking them in a covered bowl for about half an hour.

BLUE CHEESE DRESSING

MAKES 1/2 CUP

1/4 cup crumbled blue cheese

1/4 cup low-fat sour cream

2 tablespoons cholesterol-free mayonnaise

1 tablespoon extra-virgin olive oil

1 tablespoon white wine vinegar

1 teaspoon Worcestershire sauce

1/2 teaspoon minced garlic

1 teaspoon minced fresh dill (or 1/4 teaspoon dried dill weed)

1 teaspoon minced fresh summer savory (or 1/4 teaspoon dried summer savory)

1/8 teaspoon freshly ground black pepper, or to taste

Dash hot pepper sauce, or to taste

This recipe will rate top billing in your repertoire if you love the pungent flavor of blue cheese. It is decidedly rich and filling—and ideal for robust greens and main dish salads. I like to use capers, nuts, or grapes as a complementary garnish.

Place the blue cheese, sour cream, mayonnaise, olive oil, vinegar, Worcestershire sauce, and garlic in a blender; purée until smooth. Stir in the dill, summer savory, pepper, and hot pepper sauce. Taste; adjust seasonings. (If you prefer a thinner consistency, stir in some milk.) Stir before serving.

ADVANCE PREPARATION: Allow the dressing to stand for 15 to 30 minutes in the refrigerator before serving. It will keep for 2 days in a tightly closed container in the refrigerator. If it thickens after standing, thin with milk.

PER TABLESPOON: CALORIES 41 • FAT 3.7G • CHOL 3MG • SODIUM 105MG

CHUTNEY-YOGURT DRESSING

MAKES 1/2 CUP

3 tablespoons low-fat sour cream

3 tablespoons low-fat plain yogurt

2 tablespoons chutney

1 tablespoon white wine vinegar

1/4 teaspoon curry powder, or to taste

The possibilities for this dressing are almost endless, but my favorite is to drizzle it over juicy peach slices and chilled strips of broiled chicken.

In a small mixing bowl, whisk together all ingredients. Taste; adjust seasonings. Stir before serving.

ADVANCE PREPARATION: Allow this dressing to stand in the refrigerator for 15 to 30 minutes before serving. It will keep for 2 days in a tightly closed container in the refrigerator. After standing, it thickens; thin by stirring in milk or water.

PER TABLESPOON: CALORIES 14 • FAT .1G • CHOL .3MG • SODIUM 5MG

CREAMY BALSAMIC DRESSING

MAKES 1/2 CUP

1/2 cup low-fat plain yogurt

1 tablespoon balsamic vinegar

1 teaspoon low-sodium soy sauce

1 tablespoon minced fresh tarragon (or 1 teaspoon dried tarragon)

1/2 teaspoon minced garlic

1/4 teaspoon freshly ground black pepper, or to taste

Dash salt, or to taste

arragon is especially compatible with raw vegetables, particularly mushrooms, and with poultry. Try this dressing over a pretty arrangement of both atop a bed of greens.

In a small bowl, whisk together all ingredients. Taste; adjust seasonings. Stir before serving.

ADVANCE PREPARATION: If dried tarragon is used, allow the dressing to stand for 15 to 30 minutes in the refrigerator before serving. This dressing will keep for 2 days in a tightly closed container in the refrigerator. After standing, it thickens; thin by stirring in milk.

PER TABLESPOON: CALORIES 12 • FAT .2G • CHOL 1MG • SODIUM 35MG

CREAMY CURRIED GRAPEFRUIT DRESSING

MAKES 1/2 CUP

1/3 cup cholesterol-free mayonnaise

1 tablespoon frozen grapefruit juice concentrate (undiluted), thawed

1 tablespoon freshly squeezed lemon juice

1 tablespoon honey, or to taste

1/4 teaspoon curry powder

Dash freshly ground black pepper, or to taste

Here's an unusual and refreshing topping for shrimp, citrus sections, and avocado wedges arranged on a bed of greens.

In a small bowl, whisk together all ingredients. Taste; adjust seasonings. Stir before serving.

ADVANCE PREPARATION: This dressing will keep for 2 days in a tightly closed container in the refrigerator. If it thickens after standing, thin with milk.

PER TABLESPOON: CALORIES 38 • FAT 2G • CHOL 0 • SODIUM 107MG

CREAMY GOAT CHEESE DRESSING

MAKES 1/2 CUP

1/4 cup low-fat plain yogurt

3 tablespoons goat cheese (chèvre)

1 tablespoon white rice vinegar

2 teaspoons balsamic vinegar

1 teaspoon extra-virgin olive oil

1 tablespoon minced fresh basil (or 1 teaspoon dried basil)

1/4 teaspoon sugar

1/4 teaspoon freshly ground black pepper, or to taste

If you've been wondering why goat cheese has become so popular, taste this dressing—then join the fan club! In addition to being used to dress a multitude of salads, this combination makes an appetizing dip for raw vegetables or a topping to drizzle over warm steamed vegetables. If you're adventurous, try another of my tricks and pair it with beans.

In a small bowl, whisk together all ingredients. Taste; adjust seasonings. Stir before serving.

ADVANCE PREPARATION: If dried basil is used, allow the dressing to stand for 15 to 30 minutes before serving. This dressing will keep for 2 days in a tightly closed container in the refrigerator. After standing, it thickens and will need to be thinned with milk or water.

PER TABLESPOON: CALORIES 15 • FAT .8G • CHOL .4MG • SODIUM 5MG

CREAMY HERB DRESSING

<table>
<tr><td colspan="2" align="center">MAKES 1/2 CUP</td></tr>
</table>

MAKES 1/2 CUP

1/4 cup low-fat cottage cheese

2 tablespoons low-fat plain yogurt

1 tablespoon freshly squeezed lemon juice

1 tablespoon freshly grated Parmesan cheese

1 tablespoon minced shallot

1/8 teaspoon freshly ground black pepper, or to taste

1/2 teaspoon *herbes de Provence*

Dash salt, or to taste

The French herbal blend called herbes de Provence *(which includes thyme, savory, fennel, sage, rosemary, and bay leaf) is available in most gourmet shops and many supermarkets. It is the secret to the interesting blend of herbal flavors in this low-fat dressing.*

Place all ingredients, except *herbes de Provence,* in a blender; purée until smooth. Stir in pepper and herbs. Taste; adjust seasonings. Stir before serving.

ADVANCE PREPARATION: Allow the dressing to stand for 15 to 30 minutes before serving. It will keep for 2 days in a tightly closed container in the refrigerator.

PER TABLESPOON: CALORIES 14 • FAT .4G • CHOL 1MG • SODIUM 46MG

CREAMY ITALIAN DRESSING

MAKES 1/2 CUP

- 2 tablespoons low-fat cottage cheese
- 2 tablespoons low-fat plain yogurt
- 1 tablespoon extra-virgin olive oil
- 1 tablespoon tarragon white wine vinegar
- 1 tablespoon minced shallot
- 1 teaspoon Dijon mustard
- 1 teaspoon minced fresh parsley
- 1 teaspoon minced fresh basil (or 1/4 teaspoon dried basil)
- 1 teaspoon minced fresh oregano (or 1/4 teaspoon dried oregano)
- 1/4 teaspoon freshly ground black pepper, or to taste

Here is a low-fat version of the classic—all of the flavor, none of the guilt. In addition to greens and vegetables, toss this dressing with a pasta salad composed of a tubular-shaped pasta, such as mostaccioli or penne, steamed broccoli florets and zucchini, sweet red pepper, plum tomato, and any other vegetables of your choice. If you wish, include cubes of mozzarella cheese.

Place the cottage cheese, yogurt, olive oil, vinegar, shallot, and mustard in a blender; purée until smooth. Stir in the remaining ingredients. Taste; adjust seasonings. Stir before serving.

ADVANCE PREPARATION: If dried herbs are used, allow the dressing to stand for 15 to 30 minutes before serving. This dressing will keep for 2 days in a tightly closed container in the refrigerator.

PER TABLESPOON: CALORIES 22 • FAT 1.8G • CHOL .5MG • SODIUM 19MG

Tip: Since the flavor of basil (sweet basil) is so pungent, it is a good choice for dressings to be used on assertive greens. Other varieties, such as lemon basil, purple basil, and curly basil, serve different purposes and should not be substituted in the dressing recipes.

CREAMY LEMON-BASIL DRESSING

MAKES 1/2 CUP

1/3 cup low-fat plain yogurt

1 tablespoon chutney (see page 35)

1 teaspoon lemon zest

1 tablespoon freshly squeezed lemon juice

5 large basil leaves, sliced into a thin chiffonade (see page 31), about 1 tablespoon (do not substitute dried basil)

Dash freshly ground black pepper, or to taste

M̃ost often I use this dressing on thin, diagonally cut strips of broiled chicken arranged on a bed of tender greens. Accompanied with crusty bread or a fruity muffin, it makes a light and refreshing meal.

In a small bowl, whisk together all ingredients. Stir before serving.

ADVANCE PREPARATION: This dressing will keep for 2 days in a tightly closed container in the refrigerator.

PER TABLESPOON: CALORIES 12 • FAT .1G • CHOL .6MG • SODIUM 7MG

CREAMY LEMON-CAPER DRESSING

MAKES 1/2 CUP

1/4 cup cholesterol-free mayonnaise

1/4 cup freshly squeezed lemon juice

1/2 teaspoon Dijon mustard

1/2 teaspoon honey

1/2 teaspoon minced garlic

1 tablespoon minced red bell pepper

1 teaspoon capers, drained

1 teaspoon minced shallot

2 teaspoons fresh thyme leaves (or 1/2 teaspoon dried thyme)

1/8 teaspoon freshly ground black pepper, or to taste

Pinch salt, or to taste

For a razzle-dazzle entrée salad, toss this dressing with crab to create Crab Remoulade or drizzle it over a chilled poached salmon steak for do-ahead summer entertaining at its best.

In a small bowl, whisk together all ingredients. Stir before serving.

ADVANCE PREPARATION: This dressing will keep for 2 days in a tightly closed container in the refrigerator.

PER TABLESPOON: CALORIES 24 • FAT 1.5G • CHOL 0 • SODIUM 88MG

CREAMY PARMESAN-PEPPERCORN DRESSING

MAKES 1/2 CUP

- 1/3 cup low-fat cottage cheese

- 1/4 cup freshly grated Parmesan cheese

- 2 tablespoons low-fat plain yogurt

- 1 teaspoon freshly squeezed lemon juice

- 1 teaspoon tarragon vinegar

- 1/4 teaspoon minced garlic

- 1/4 teaspoon freshly ground black pepper (coarse grind), or to taste

This hearty, rich-tasting dressing can be prepared quickly in your blender using ingredients you are likely to have on hand.

Place all ingredients in a blender. Purée until smooth and creamy. Taste; adjust seasonings. Stir before serving.

ADVANCE PREPARATION: This dressing will keep for 2 days in a tightly closed container in the refrigerator. After standing, it thickens; thin by stirring in milk.

PER TABLESPOON: CALORIES 25 • FAT 1.2G • CHOL 3MG • SODIUM 99MG

Tip: Freshly ground or cracked peppercorns are preferable to preground because the peppercorn releases much of its oil in the form of aroma and flavor. For coarse chunks of pepper, crack peppercorns by pressing them firmly on a cutting board with the side of a French chef's knife.

CREAMY PEANUT DRESSING

MAKES 1/2 CUP

2 tablespoons hoisin sauce (see tip)

2 tablespoons low-fat plain yogurt

2 tablespoons water (more may be necessary if peanut butter is very thick)

1 tablespoon smooth peanut butter

1/2 teaspoon dark sesame oil (see page 6)

1/2 teaspoon chili paste with garlic, or to taste (see tip)

Peanut butter combined with the Asian flavors of hoisin sauce and sesame oil creates a highly flavored topping for a pasta and vegetable salad, sautéed chicken strips on a bed of greens, or simply greens and vegetables.

In a small bowl, whisk together all ingredients. Taste; adjust seasonings. If you prefer a thinner consistency, add water. Stir before serving.

ADVANCE PREPARATION: This dressing will keep for 2 days in a tightly closed container in the refrigerator. After standing, it thickens; thin by stirring in water.

PER TABLESPOON: CALORIES 19 • FAT 1.4G • CHOL .2MG • SODIUM 44MG

Tip: Chili paste with garlic, also known as Chinese chili sauce or chili purée, is a hot, spicy sauce made from soybeans, hot peppers, rice vinegar, salt, oil, and garlic. Store it in a tightly closed container in the refrigerator.

Tip: Chinese hoisin sauce, found in the oriental section of supermarkets and in specialty stores, is a thick, sweet, reddish-brown sauce usually made from soybeans, vinegar, chilies, spices, and garlic. The sweetness varies from one brand to another. Refrigerated in a tightly closed container, it will keep almost indefinitely. There is no substitute.

CREAMY PESTO DRESSING

<table>
<tr><td>

MAKES 1/2 CUP

2 tablespoons Basil Pesto
(page 137)

2 tablespoons low-fat plain
yogurt

2 tablespoons garlic-infused
extra-virgin olive oil (or
2 tablespoons extra-virgin
olive oil plus a dash of
minced garlic, to taste)

2 tablespoons white wine
vinegar

1/4 teaspoon freshly
ground black pepper
(coarse grind), or to taste

</td></tr>
</table>

Using Basil Pesto, you can quickly create this dressing to enhance a wide array of salads, from fish and shellfish to chicken or pasta with vegetables. Garnish your salad with freshly grated Parmesan cheese, freshly ground black pepper, and a sprig of fresh basil.

In a small bowl, whisk together all ingredients. Taste; adjust seasonings. Stir before serving.

ADVANCE PREPARATION: This dressing will keep for 2 days in a tightly closed container in the refrigerator. If it thickens after standing, thin with milk or water.

PER TABLESPOON: CALORIES 51 • FAT 5.3G • CHOL .2MG • SODIUM 4MG

CREAMY POTATO SALAD DRESSING

MAKES 1/2 CUP

- 2 tablespoons cholesterol-free mayonnaise
- 2 tablespoons low-fat plain yogurt
- 2 tablespoons minced scallion (white part), or to taste
- 1 tablespoon yellow mustard
- 1 tablespoon skim milk
- 1 tablespoon juice from sweet pickles
- 1 tablespoon minced fresh parsley
- 1 teaspoon sugar
- 1/4 teaspoon celery seed
- 1/4 teaspoon freshly ground black pepper, or to taste
- Dash paprika, or to taste
- Dash salt, or to taste

This can serve as your basic dressing for potato salad. I make mine with unpeeled boiled new potatoes, chopped celery, carrots, scallions, and hard-cooked eggs. The recipe is an updated, lean, and healthful version of the dressing my mom has used for 50 years!

In a small bowl, whisk together all ingredients. Taste; adjust seasonings. Stir before tossing with potato salad ingredients. If you prefer a thinner dressing, stir in more milk or half-and-half.

ADVANCE PREPARATION: This dressing will keep for 2 days in a tightly closed container in the refrigerator. After tossing it with potatoes, allow the salad to stand in the refrigerator for at least an hour before serving.

PER TABLESPOON: CALORIES 18 • FAT .9G • CHOL .3MG • SODIUM 73MG

CREAMY TARRAGON-DIJON DRESSING

MAKES 1/2 CUP

- 1/4 cup extra-virgin olive oil
- 2 tablespoons cholesterol-free mayonnaise
- 2 tablespoons red wine vinegar
- 1 teaspoon Dijon mustard
- 2 teaspoons minced fresh tarragon (or 1/2 teaspoon dried tarragon)
- 1/8 teaspoon freshly ground black pepper, or to taste

There is something special about this dressing drizzled over chilled crisp-tender asparagus spears arranged on a bed of greens. To turn the salad into an entrée, I also add shrimp, chunks of mild fish, or even canned tuna.

In a small bowl, whisk together all ingredients. Taste; adjust seasonings. Stir or shake before serving.

ADVANCE PREPARATION: If dried tarragon is used, allow the dressing to stand for 15 to 30 minutes before serving. This dressing will keep for 2 days in a tightly closed container in the refrigerator.

PER TABLESPOON: CALORIES 70 • FAT 7.5G • CHOL 0 • SODIUM 42MG

CREAMY TOMATO DRESSING

MAKES 1/2 CUP

2 tablespoons tomato paste
(see tip)

2 tablespoons extra-virgin
olive oil

2 tablespoons red wine
vinegar

1 tablespoon cholesterol-
free mayonnaise

1 tablespoon water

1/2 teaspoon minced garlic

1/4 teaspoon sugar

1/8 teaspoon freshly
ground black pepper, or
to taste

Dash salt, or to taste

Easy and exceptionally quick and simple to prepare, this dressing will add a special touch to shrimp, green beans, or potatoes.

In a small bowl, whisk together all ingredients, making certain the sugar is dissolved. Taste; adjust seasonings. Stir before serving.

ADVANCE PREPARATION: This dressing will keep for 2 days in a tightly closed container in the refrigerator. After standing, it thickens; thin by stirring in water.

PER TABLESPOON: CALORIES 39 • FAT 3.8G • CHOL 0 • SODIUM 23MG

Tip: Tomato paste is available in tubes at many supermarkets and specialty stores, ideal for recipes calling for less than a 6-ounce can.

CREAMY YOGURT DRESSING

MAKES 1/2 CUP

1/3 cup low-fat plain yogurt

1 tablespoon freshly squeezed lemon juice

1 tablespoon white rice vinegar

1 teaspoon light brown sugar

1/2 teaspoon Dijon mustard

1/8 teaspoon minced garlic

1/8 teaspoon freshly ground black pepper, or to taste

Besides using this dressing on your green salads, think of it when you need a dip for raw or steamed vegetables.

In a small bowl, whisk together all ingredients. Taste; adjust seasonings. Whisk or shake before serving.

ADVANCE PREPARATION: This dressing will keep for 2 days in a tightly closed container in the refrigerator.

PER TABLESPOON: CALORIES **9** • FAT **.2G** • CHOL **.6MG** • SODIUM **8MG**

CUCUMBER-DILL DRESSING

MAKES 1/2 CUP

1/2 cup chopped cucumber (cucumber should be peeled and seeded; or just peeled if an English cucumber is used—see tip)

2 tablespoons low-fat plain yogurt

1 teaspoon fresh lemon juice

1/4 teaspoon minced garlic

1/4 teaspoon sugar

Dash white pepper, or to taste

1 tablespoon fresh dill (or 1/2 teaspoon dried dill weed)

ince this fat-free dressing is light and mild in flavor, it is best served on tender and delicate greens, such as butterhead lettuce, to create a cool and refreshing salad.

Place all ingredients, except dill, in a blender. Purée until smooth. Stir in dill. Taste; adjust seasonings. Chill. Stir before serving.

ADVANCE PREPARATION: If dried dill weed is used, allow the dressing to stand for 15 to 30 minutes before serving. With either form of dill, if possible allow time for the dressing to chill before serving. It will keep for up to 2 days in a tightly closed container in the refrigerator.

PER TABLESPOON: CALORIES 4 • FAT .1G • CHOL .2MG • SODIUM 3MG

Tip: An English or European (hothouse) cucumber has a thinner skin and fewer seeds than a standard garden cucumber.

CURRIED YOGURT DRESSING

<table>
<tr><td>

MAKES **1/2** CUP

1/4 cup low-fat plain yogurt

2 tablespoons cholesterol-free mayonnaise

2 tablespoons white rice vinegar

1 teaspoon curry powder, or to taste

1/4 teaspoon sugar

1/4 teaspoon paprika

1/4 teaspoon chili powder

Dash salt, or to taste

</td></tr>
</table>

particularly like this dressing tossed with a mixture of winter fruit and crunchy vegetables such as apples, pears, green grapes, celery, and bean sprouts. Or try it tossed with chunks of chicken and garnish with raisins.

In a small mixing bowl, stir together the ingredients. Taste; adjust seasonings. Stir before serving.

ADVANCE PREPARATION: Allow this dressing to stand in the refrigerator for 15 to 30 minutes before serving. It will keep for 2 days in a tightly closed container in the refrigerator.

PER TABLESPOON: CALORIES 17 • FAT .9G • CHOL .4MG • SODIUM 46MG

Tip: A blend of herbs and spices, imported curries are often more intense in flavor than domestic ones. The amount to add may vary depending on the type of curry powder you use, as well as your personal taste. If you do not plan to serve the dressing right away, be aware that the curry flavor becomes stronger when allowed to stand.

GREEK FETA CHEESE DRESSING

MAKES 1/2 CUP

1/4 cup crumbled mild
feta cheese

3 tablespoons low-fat plain
yogurt

1 tablespoon freshly
squeezed lemon juice

2 teaspoons minced fresh
mint (or 1/4 teaspoon
dried marjoram)

2 teaspoons minced fresh
oregano (or 1/4 teaspoon
dried oregano)

1/2 teaspoon minced garlic

1/8 teaspoon freshly
ground black pepper, or
to taste

This will add a special touch to an otherwise boring bowl of lettuce and tomato wedges. Toss in a few Greek olives and peppers for a true Greek experience.

In a small bowl, whisk together all ingredients. Taste; adjust seasonings. Stir before serving.

ADVANCE PREPARATION: If dried herbs are used, allow the dressing to stand for 15 to 30 minutes before serving. This dressing will keep for 2 days in a tightly closed container in the refrigerator. After standing, it thickens; thin by stirring in milk.

PER TABLESPOON: CALORIES 15 • FAT 1G • CHOL 4MG • SODIUM 51MG

GREEN GODDESS DRESSING

MAKES 1/2 CUP
1/3 cup low-fat sour cream
1 tablespoon extra-virgin olive oil
1 tablespoon tarragon white wine vinegar
1 teaspoon freshly squeezed lemon juice
2 teaspoons chopped anchovies (about 4 flat anchovy fillets)
1/2 teaspoon minced garlic
1 scallion (both green and white parts), chopped
1 tablespoon minced fresh parsley
2 teaspoons minced fresh tarragon (or 1/2 teaspoon dried tarragon)
1/8 teaspoon freshly ground black pepper, or to taste

Here's my version of the classic so popular for serving with seafood and vegetable salads. For variety, try this rich, thick, creamy, and bold dressing in potato salad.

Place all ingredients in a blender; purée until smooth. Taste; adjust seasonings. Whisk or shake before serving.

ADVANCE PREPARATION: This dressing will keep for 2 days in a tightly closed container in the refrigerator. After standing, it thickens; thin by stirring in water or milk.

PER TABLESPOON: CALORIES 20 • FAT 1.9G • CHOL 2MG • SODIUM 74MG

HERBED TAHINI DRESSING

MAKES 1/2 CUP

2 tablespoons tahini
(sesame butter)

1/4 teaspoon grated lemon
rind

2 tablespoons freshly
squeezed lemon juice

2 tablespoons water (more
may be necessary if tahini
is very thick)

1 tablespoon low-fat plain
yogurt

1 tablespoon safflower oil

1 teaspoon honey, or to
taste

1 tablespoon minced fresh
parsley

1 teaspoon minced fresh
chives (do not substitute
dried chives; if unavail-
able, substitute minced
scallion greens)

1/2 teaspoon minced garlic

1/8 teaspoon freshly
ground black pepper, or
to taste

This flavorful dressing is a good choice to dress up a simple salad of spinach and sliced mushrooms.

In a small bowl, whisk together all ingredients, beating until smooth. Taste; adjust seasonings. Stir before serving.

ADVANCE PREPARATION: This dressing will keep for up to 2 days in a tightly closed container in the refrigerator. After standing, it thickens; thin by stirring in water.

PER TABLESPOON: CALORIES 43 • FAT 1.7G • CHOL .1MG • SODIUM 2MG

Tip: Tahini, or sesame butter, is a nutty-tasting paste made from raw, unhulled sesame seeds. Stir in the oils before using and re-frigerate the jar after opening.

HOISIN DRESSING

<table>
<tr><td colspan="1">MAKES 1/2 CUP</td></tr>
</table>

MAKES 1/2 CUP

3 tablespoons hoisin sauce
(see page 95)

3 tablespoons freshly
squeezed lemon juice

3 tablespoons safflower oil

1 tablespoon dark sesame
oil (see page 6)

1 1/2 teaspoons sugar, or
to taste

This thick, smooth dressing is delicious on greens topped with crunchy, mild oriental vegetables such as Chinese pea pods and bok choy. For a special treat, try it drizzled over shrimp.

In a small bowl, whisk together all ingredients, making certain the sugar is dissolved. Stir before serving.

Note: Hoisin sauces vary in sweetness; adjust sugar accordingly.

ADVANCE PREPARATION: This dressing will keep for 2 days in a tightly closed container in the refrigerator.

PER TABLESPOON: CALORIES 69 • FAT 6.9G • CHOL 0 • SODIUM 48MG

HONEY-DIJON DRESSING

MAKES 1/2 CUP

1/4 cup cholesterol-free
mayonnaise

1 tablespoon honey
(2 tablespoons if you
prefer a sweeter flavor)

1 tablespoon low-fat plain
yogurt

1 tablespoon freshly
squeezed lemon juice

1 tablespoon Dijon
mustard

1/4 teaspoon poppy seeds

Dash freshly ground black
pepper

In addition to being used to spark up a salad, this dressing can be heated gently and used as a warm sauce over steamed vegetables. Chilled, it makes an appetizing dip for raw vegetables.

In a small bowl, whisk together all ingredients. Stir before serving.

ADVANCE PREPARATION: This dressing will keep for 2 days in a tightly closed container in the refrigerator. After standing, it thickens; thin by stirring in milk or water.

PER TABLESPOON: CALORIES 30 • FAT 1.6G • CHOL .1MG • SODIUM 86MG

INDONESIAN PEANUT DRESSING

MAKES 1/2 CUP

1/4 cup peanut butter (smooth or chunky)

2 tablespoons water (more if the peanut butter is very thick)

2 tablespoons white rice vinegar

1 tablespoon safflower oil

1/2 teaspoon low-sodium soy sauce

1/2 teaspoon dark sesame oil (see page 6)

1/2 teaspoon minced garlic

1/4 teaspoon crushed red pepper, or to taste

This spicy dressing shines best when tossed with a variety of vegetables such as julienned celery, shredded carrots, thinly sliced cucumber, broccoli and cauliflower florets, fresh bean sprouts, and thin wedges of plum tomatoes. Or use it as a dip for raw vegetables.

In a small bowl, whisk together all ingredients. Taste; adjust seasonings. Stir before serving.

ADVANCE PREPARATION: This dressing will keep for 1 week in a tightly closed container in the refrigerator. After standing, it thickens; thin by stirring in water.

PER TABLESPOON: CALORIES 66 • FAT 6G • CHOL 0 • SODIUM 56MG

LEMON CAESAR DRESSING

MAKES 1/2 CUP

1/4 cup freshly squeezed
lemon juice

2 tablespoons low-fat plain
yogurt

2 tablespoons cholesterol-
free mayonnaise

2 tablespoons minced fresh
parsley

1 tablespoon freshly grated
Parmesan cheese

1/2 teaspoon
Worcestershire sauce

1/2 teaspoon minced garlic

1/8 teaspoon freshly
ground black pepper, or
to taste

Dash salt, or to taste

Few drops hot pepper
sauce, or to taste

You've been asking for a light version of the classic. Here it is—equally as delicious but with a mere fraction of the fat and cholesterol. Enjoy!

In a small mixing bowl, whisk together the ingredients. Taste; adjust seasonings. Stir before serving.

ADVANCE PREPARATION: This dressing will keep for 2 days in a tightly closed container in the refrigerator.

PER TABLESPOON: CALORIES 19 • FAT 1G • CHOL .8MG • SODIUM 61MG

Tip: Eggs in undercooked or raw form now carry a risk of salmonellosis (salmonella-caused food poisoning). For this reason, none of the dressings in this book call for raw eggs.

ORANGE TAHINI DRESSING

MAKES 1/2 CUP

1/4 cup freshly squeezed orange juice

1/4 cup tahini (sesame butter)

1 tablespoon freshly squeezed lemon juice

1 teaspoon low–sodium soy sauce

1 teaspoon honey

1/4 teaspoon minced garlic

Since the flavor of tahini is robust, this dressing pairs especially well with bold vegetables such as broccoli and pungent greens such as sorrel and arugula.

In a small bowl, whisk together all ingredients. Stir before serving.

ADVANCE PREPARATION: This dressing will keep for 2 days in a tightly closed container in the refrigerator.

PER TABLESPOON: CALORIES 52 • FAT .02G • CHOL 0 • SODIUM 25MG

PARSLEY-CUCUMBER DRESSING

MAKES 1/2 CUP
1/4 cup chopped cucumber, peeled and seeded (or just peeled if an English cucumber is used—see tip on page 101)
1/4 cup fresh parsley sprigs
1/4 cup minced scallion, green parts
2 tablespoons low-fat plain yogurt
1 tablespoon lite ricotta cheese
1 tablespoon freshly squeezed lemon juice
1/2 teaspoon minced garlic
1/4 teaspoon sugar
1/8 teaspoon freshly ground black pepper, or to taste
Dash salt

No single flavor predominates, but the blend is magic in this low-fat dressing.

Place all ingredients in a blender; purée until smooth. Taste; adjust seasonings. Whisk or shake before serving.

ADVANCE PREPARATION: Before serving, refrigerate this dressing for 30 minutes to allow the flavors to blend. It will keep for 2 days in a tightly closed container in the refrigerator.

PER TABLESPOON: CALORIES 8 • FAT .2G • CHOL .8MG • SODIUM 5.8MG

RANCH DRESSING

MAKES 1/2 CUP

1/4 cup low-fat cottage cheese

1/4 cup low-fat buttermilk

1 tablespoon freshly squeezed lemon juice

1 teaspoon minced shallot

1/4 teaspoon Dijon mustard

1 teaspoon minced fresh oregano (or 1/4 teaspoon dried oregano)

1 teaspoon fresh thyme leaves (or 1/4 teaspoon dried thyme)

1/8 teaspoon freshly ground black pepper, or to taste

Dash salt, or to taste

This dressing won't trouble the calorie-conscious, yet it is rich tasting and flavorful enough to please the most particular connoisseur.

Place the cottage cheese, buttermilk, lemon juice, shallot, and mustard in a blender; purée until smooth. Stir in the remaining ingredients. Taste; adjust seasonings. Stir before serving.

ADVANCE PREPARATION: If dried herbs are used, allow the dressing to stand for 15 to 30 minutes before serving. This dressing will keep for 2 days in a tightly closed container in the refrigerator.

PER TABLESPOON: CALORIES **10** • FAT **.2**G • CHOL **.9**MG • SODIUM **37**MG

RICOTTA-CHIVE DRESSING

MAKES 1/2 CUP

1/4 cup lite ricotta cheese

2 tablespoons low-fat plain yogurt

2 tablespoons white wine vinegar

2 tablespoons minced fresh chives (do not substitute dried chives; if unavailable, substitute minced scallion greens)

1/4 teaspoon minced garlic

1/8 teaspoon freshly ground black pepper, or to taste

No oil is added to this dressing, so the fat content is enticingly low! Allow the flavors to blend for an hour or so before serving, then enjoy it on a mixture of gourmet greens.

Place all ingredients in a blender; purée until smooth. Taste, adjust seasonings. Whisk or shake before serving.

ADVANCE PREPARATION: Allow this dressing to stand in the refrigerator for about 30 minutes before serving. It will keep for 2 days in a tightly closed container in the refrigerator.

PER TABLESPOON: CALORIES 14 • FAT .7G • CHOL 3MG • SODIUM 12MG

Tip: Avoid dried chopped chives, which have lost their characteristic flavor and aroma. Wrap whole fresh chives in damp paper towels, seal in a plastic bag, and refrigerate. If fresh chives are unavailable, julienned strips of scallion greens can be substituted.

TAHINI–POPPY SEED DRESSING

<table>
<tr><td>

MAKES 1/2 CUP

3 tablespoons tahini
 (sesame butter)

2 tablespoons white rice
 vinegar

1 tablespoon safflower oil

1 tablespoon water (more
 may be necessary if tahini
 is very thick)

1 tablespoon honey

1/2 teaspoon poppy seeds

</td></tr>
</table>

As well as being an unusual salad dressing, this slightly sweet tahini mixture makes a delicious dip for raw vegetables.

In a small bowl, whisk together all ingredients. Stir before serving.

ADVANCE PREPARATION: This dressing will keep for 1 week in a tightly closed container in the refrigerator. After standing, it thickens; thin by stirring in water.

PER TABLESPOON: CALORIES 58 • FAT 1.8G • CHOL 0 • SODIUM .2MG

THOUSAND ISLAND DRESSING

MAKES 1/2 CUP

1/4 cup cholesterol-free mayonnaise

2 tablespoons ketchup

1 tablespoon freshly squeezed lemon juice

1 tablespoon minced onion

1 tablespoon minced red bell pepper

1 tablespoon minced fresh parsley

1 tablespoon sweet pickle relish

Pinch cayenne pepper, or to taste

This homemade version of the rich, thick American classic somehow still seems most appropriate served on a thick wedge of iceberg lettuce, just as it was in the 1950s.

In a small bowl, whisk together all ingredients. Taste; adjust seasonings. Stir before serving.

ADVANCE PREPARATION: If possible, allow this dressing to stand in the refrigerator for 15 to 30 minutes before serving. It will keep for 2 days in a tightly closed container in the refrigerator. If it thickens or if you prefer a thinner consistency, thin by stirring in milk.

PER TABLESPOON: CALORIES 28 • FAT 1.5G • CHOL 0 • SODIUM 146MG

VARIATION:
* for a zestier flavor, for the ketchup substitute 2 tablespoons chili sauce, or to taste

Tip: Refrigerated onions tend not to release the tear-producing vapors as much as those stored at room temperature.

WATERCRESS DRESSING

MAKES 1/2 CUP

1/4 cup low-fat plain yogurt

2 tablespoons white wine vinegar

1/8 teaspoon freshly ground black pepper, or to taste

2 drops hot pepper sauce, or to taste

Pinch dry mustard powder

1/4 cup coarsely chopped fresh watercress leaves

The clean, fresh, peppery taste of watercress inspired this springtime dressing. I like to serve it over warm poached salmon steaks and crisp-tender new asparagus arranged on a bed of greens. Because watercress is highly perishable, quickly turning yellow and losing flavor, buy it fresh the day you plan to make this dressing.

In a small bowl, whisk together all ingredients except watercress. Stir in the watercress. Stir again before serving.

ADVANCE PREPARATION: Allow this dressing to stand in the refrigerator 15 to 30 minutes before serving. It will keep for a day in a tightly closed container in the refrigerator.

PER TABLESPOON: CALORIES 5 • FAT .1G • CHOL .4MG • SODIUM 5MG

FRUIT DRESSINGS

ALTHOUGH MANY OF the dressings in the previous two chapters can be used on fruit salads, the recipes in this section are specifically designed to enhance the special qualities of fruit.

Some are sweet and spirited by the addition of honey, sugar, maple syrup, juice concentrates, or sweet liqueurs such as Grand Marnier or Amaretto. Others call on ingredients such as lime juice and plain yogurt to create a tart and lively piquancy. When paired with fruits, you can count on these dressings to produce unexpectedly delightful combinations. Some can be paired with other foods as well (see the charts on pages 143–49). As with the other creamy dressings, ingredient substitutions can be made, such as crème fraîche for whipping cream or sour cream for yogurt (see "Ingredients for Smooth, Creamy Texture" on pages 12–14).

Always make these fruit dressings with fresh ingredients, especially the dairy products and juices. These dressings will keep in the refrigerator for a day or two. Serve them chilled, and always stir or shake before using.

Here are some tips for creating your fruit salads:

- For the best flavor, always use fruit at the peak of its ripeness.
- Since the sweetness of fruits varies, it sometimes may be necessary to adjust the amount of sweetener in the dressing.
- Don't overlook the addition of sour fruits; they will provide an appealing tartness.
- Consider cutting the fruit into interesting shapes: cubes, wedges, slices, fingers, or balls.
- Leave the skins on fruit for color as well as for fiber.
- The addition of fish or shellfish will turn the salad into a more substantial entrée, especially when accompanied by breadsticks or muffins.
- Try serving a fruit salad to cleanse the palate between courses of a meal or as a dessert at the end of a rich and filling meal.

AMARETTO DRESSING

MAKE 1/2 CUP
1/3 cup whipping cream
2 tablespoons Amaretto
1/4 cup ground blanched almonds
1 tablespoon sugar

liced fresh pears or peaches become a sophisticated dessert with a drizzle of this dressing. Or try it over fruit atop a slice of angel food cake or pound cake.

In a small bowl, beat the whipping cream until soft peaks form. Fold in the remaining ingredients. Taste; adjust seasonings. Refrigerate at least 1 hour to blend flavors. Stir before serving.

ADVANCE PREPARATION: This dressing will keep for a day in a tightly closed container in the refrigerator.

PER TABLESPOON: CALORIES **76** • FAT **5.8G** • CHOL **14MG** • SODIUM **4MG**

VARIATION:
- for the whipping cream, substitute crème fraîche (use as is, no need to whip)

BERRY DRESSING WITH POPPY SEEDS

1/4 cup low-fat plain
yogurt

1/3 cup sliced strawberries
(about 3 medium-size
strawberries)

1 tablespoon raspberry
vinegar (or blueberry or
black currant vinegar)

1 tablespoon honey, or
to taste

1/2 teaspoon poppy seeds

This dressing is the perfect partner for a bowl of fresh fruit. I also use it to top a summer salad of greens tossed with strawberries, grapes, and sliced almonds.

Place all ingredients, except poppy seeds, in a blender. Purée until smooth. Stir in poppy seeds. Chill. Stir before serving.

ADVANCE PREPARATION: This dressing will keep for a day in a tightly closed container in the refrigerator.

PER TABLESPOON: CALORIES 15 • FAT .2G • CHOL .4MG • SODIUM 5MG

CREAMY MAPLE SAUCE

MAKES 1/2 CUP
1/2 cup low-fat plain yogurt
2 tablespoons pure maple syrup
1/2 teaspoon poppy seeds

This uncomplicated fruit sauce takes only seconds to make, but it is guaranteed to glorify fresh fruit, especially when drizzled over orange segments.

In a small bowl, stir together all ingredients. Chill. Stir before serving.

ADVANCE PREPARATION: This dressing will keep for 2 days in a tightly closed container in the refrigerator.

PER TABLESPOON: CALORIES 13 • FAT .3G • CHOL .9MG • SODIUM 10MG

CREAMY ORANGE CURRY DRESSING

MAKES 1/2 CUP
1/4 cup low-fat plain yogurt
2 tablespoons orange marmalade
2 tablespoons freshly squeezed orange juice
2 teaspoons Dijon mustard
1/2 teaspoon curry powder, or to taste

This sweet-savory dressing goes well over pear slices; top with chopped pecans.

In a small bowl, whisk together all ingredients. Chill. Stir before serving.

ADVANCE PREPARATION: This dressing will keep for 2 days in a tightly closed container in the refrigerator. After standing, it thickens; thin with orange juice.

PER TABLESPOON: CALORIES 21 • FAT .1G • CHOL .4MG • SODIUM 9MG

CREAMY PAPAYA DRESSING

MAKES 1/2 CUP
1 cup 1/2-inch cubes of papaya (about 1 papaya)
1/2 teaspoon lime zest
2 tablespoons freshly squeezed lime juice
2 tablespoons low-fat plain yogurt
1 tablespoon honey, or to taste

For the best flavor and texture, be sure your papaya is at the peak of its ripeness and juiciness!

Place all ingredients, except lime zest, in a blender. Purée until smooth. Stir in lime zest. Chill. Stir before serving.

ADVANCE PREPARATION: This dressing will keep for a day in a tightly closed container in the refrigerator. If it thickens after standing, thin by stirring in water or orange juice.

PER TABLESPOON: CALORIES **18** • FAT **.1**G • CHOL **.2**MG • SODIUM **3**MG

FLUFFY ORANGE DRESSING

<table>
<tr><td>MAKES 1/2 CUP</td></tr>
</table>

1/3 cup whipping cream

3 tablespoons frozen orange juice concentrate (undiluted), thawed

1 teaspoon honey, or to taste

Dash nutmeg, or to taste

This thick, rich dressing can also be used as a dip for fresh fruit or as a topping for a light cake such as angel food.

In a small bowl, beat the whipping cream until soft peaks form. Fold in the remaining ingredients. Taste; adjust seasonings. Refrigerate at least an hour to blend flavors. Stir before serving.

ADVANCE PREPARATION: This dressing will keep for 2 days in a tightly closed container in the refrigerator.

PER TABLESPOON: CALORIES 45 • FAT 3.7G • CHOL 14MG • SODIUM 4MG

VARIATION:
- for the whipping cream, substitute $1/3$ cup crème fraîche (use as is, no need to whip)

Tip: In its freshly ground form, nutmeg is more aromatic and more flavorful than preground nutmeg. When grinding, the entire nutmeg is usable. Stored in a jar in your spice cabinet, whole nutmeg will keep its flavor for years.

GINGERED YOGURT

MAKES 1/2 CUP

1/2 cup low-fat plain yogurt

1 tablespoon honey, or to taste

2 teaspoons coarsely chopped crystallized ginger, or to taste

1/2 teaspoon curry powder, or to taste

This recipe calls for crystallized (candied) ginger, which is dried ginger coated with crystallized sugar. It lends a different flavor than fresh gingerroot; they are not interchangeable. Use the recipe as is or as a guide, adjusting the flavors to suit your own taste. In addition to drizzling this sauce over balls of honeydew and cantaloupe, it is also delicious tossed with a mixture of fresh bean sprouts, chopped celery, water chestnuts, mandarin oranges, and chunks of pineapple.

Place all ingredients in a blender. Purée until smooth, making certain the crystallized ginger is completely blended in. Chill. Stir before serving.

ADVANCE PREPARATION: This dressing will keep for 2 days in a tightly closed container in the refrigerator.

PER TABLESPOON: CALORIES 18 • FAT .2G • CHOL .9MG • SODIUM 10MG

HONEY AND YOGURT DRESSING

MAKES 1/2 CUP

1/3 cup low-fat plain
   yogurt

1 tablespoon honey

1 tablespoon freshly
   squeezed lemon juice

1/4 teaspoon celery seed

Dash paprika

This sweet dressing is especially appropriate for fresh fruit salads.

In a small bowl, stir together all ingredients. Chill. Stir before serving.

ADVANCE PREPARATION: This dressing will keep for 2 days in a tightly closed container in the refrigerator.

PER TABLESPOON: CALORIES 15 • FAT .2G • CHOL .6MG • SODIUM 7MG

HONEY-LIME DRESSING

MAKES 1/2 CUP
1/4 cup low-fat plain yogurt
1/2 teaspoon lime zest
3 tablespoons freshly squeezed lime juice
1 tablespoon honey, or to taste
1/2 teaspoon poppy seeds

Drizzle this creamy dressing over an artistically arranged platter of fresh fruit and serve as a salad course or as dessert.

In a small bowl, stir together all ingredients. Chill. Stir before serving.

ADVANCE PREPARATION: This dressing will keep for 2 days in a tightly closed container in the refrigerator.

PER TABLESPOON: CALORIES 15 • FAT .2G • CHOL .4MG • SODIUM 5MG

Tip: When either grating or zesting citrus rind, remove only the outer colored part; the white portion beneath tends to be bitter.

LEMON-MINT DRESSING

MAKES 1/2 CUP

1/3 cup low-fat plain
yogurt

1/2 teaspoon grated lemon
rind

2 tablespoons freshly
squeezed lemon juice

1 teaspoon honey, or
to taste

1 tablespoon minced fresh
mint (do not substitute
dried mint)

This splendid sauce can turn a bowl of summer fruit into a special indulgence. Adjust the amount of honey to suit your taste. Or omit the honey and the grated lemon rind; for the freshly squeezed lemon juice, substitute 2 tablespoons undiluted, thawed frozen lemonade concentrate.

In a small bowl, whisk together all ingredients. Chill. Stir before serving.

ADVANCE PREPARATION: This dressing will keep for 2 days in a tightly closed container in the refrigerator.

PER TABLESPOON: CALORIES 10 • FAT .2G • CHOL .6MG • SODIUM 7MG

MAPLE-WALNUT DRESSING

<table>
<tr><td colspan="2" align="center">MAKES 1/2 CUP</td></tr>
<tr><td colspan="2">

1/4 cup low-fat sour cream

1 tablespoon cholesterol-free mayonnaise

2 tablespoons pure maple syrup

1 tablespoon freshly squeezed lemon juice

1 tablespoon chopped walnuts

1/4 teaspoon celery seed

1/4 teaspoon dry mustard powder

Dash paprika

Dash salt

</td></tr>
</table>

Toss this dressing with chunks of crisp apples for a sensational Waldorf salad; or use it as a dip for apple and pear slices.

In a small mixing bowl, stir together all ingredients. Stir before serving.

ADVANCE PREPARATION: This dressing will keep for 2 days in a tightly closed container in the refrigerator.

PER TABLESPOON: CALORIES 10 • FAT .7G • CHOL 0 • SODIUM 20MG

MINTED CHUTNEY-LIME SAUCE

MAKES 1/2 CUP

1/3 cup low-fat plain
yogurt

1 tablespoon lime zest

1 tablespoon freshly
squeezed lime juice

1 tablespoon chutney

1 tablespoon chiffonade
(see page 31) of fresh mint
(do not substitute dried
mint)

This sauce will glorify an ordinary wedge of honeydew melon. Garnished with a wedge of lime and a sprig of fresh mint, it becomes an attractive and refreshing dessert or snack—or try it at breakfast.

In a small bowl, stir together all ingredients. Chill. Stir before serving.

ADVANCE PREPARATION: This dressing will keep for 2 days in a tightly closed container in the refrigerator.

PER TABLESPOON: CALORIES 12 • FAT .2G • CHOL .6MG • SODIUM 7MG

NECTARINE DRESSING

<table>
<tr><td colspan="2" align="center">MAKES 1/2 CUP</td></tr>
<tr><td>

1 medium-size nectarine, peeled, seeded, and sliced

3 tablespoons orange juice

1 tablespoon honey, or to taste

Dash cinnamon

</td></tr>
</table>

ake this when nectarines are at their juiciest and best!

Place all ingredients in a blender; purée until smooth. Taste; adjust seasonings. Chill. Stir before serving.

ADVANCE PREPARATION: This dressing should be served within an hour or two after being made.

PER TABLESPOON: CALORIES **19** • FAT **.1G** • CHOL **0** • SODIUM **.2MG**

ORANGE LIQUEUR FRUIT SAUCE

MAKES 1/2 CUP

1/3 cup whipping cream

2 tablespoons Grand Marnier or Triple Sec

1 tablespoon frozen orange juice concentrate (undiluted), thawed

1 tablespoon light brown sugar

1 teaspoon orange zest

Here is the ultimate in simple elegance and superb taste. For a special dessert, use this sauce to top fresh strawberries; garnish with semisweet chocolate shavings. The sauce also can be poured over angel food cake and fruit or can be used as a dip for fresh fruit.

In a small bowl, beat the whipping cream until soft peaks form. Fold in the remaining ingredients. Taste; adjust seasonings. Stir before serving.

ADVANCE PREPARATION: Before serving, refrigerate this dressing for 1 hour to allow the flavors to blend. It will keep for a day in a tightly closed container in the refrigerator.

PER TABLESPOON: CALORIES 56 • FAT 3.7G • CHOL 14MG • SODIUM 4MG

VARIATION:

- for the whipping cream, substitute $1/3$ cup crème fraîche (use as is, no need to whip)

PEANUT BUTTER–ORANGE FRUIT SAUCE

MAKES 1/2 CUP

3 tablespoons freshly
squeezed orange juice

2 tablespoons freshly
squeezed lemon juice

2 tablespoons smooth
peanut butter (it may be
necessary to add a little
water if peanut butter is
very thick)

1 tablespoon honey, or to
taste

Dash freshly ground black
pepper, or to taste

The surprise addition of peanut butter turns this simple mixture into an unforgettable fruit topping. Kids love it, too!

In a small bowl, whisk together all ingredients. Taste; adjust seasonings. Stir before serving.

ADVANCE PREPARATION: This dressing will keep for 2 days in a tightly closed container in the refrigerator.

PER TABLESPOON: CALORIES 35 • FAT 2G • CHOL 0 • SODIUM 19MG

Tip: Peanut butter is best when it is the natural variety, with the oil on top; stir in the oil before using. Many of the processed peanut butters are hydrogenated to prevent separation and have sugar, salt, and stabilizers added.

STRAWBERRY-MINT VINAIGRETTE

MAKES 1/2 CUP
1/2 cup sliced strawberries (about 5 medium-size strawberries)
2 tablespoons black currant vinegar (or raspberry vinegar)
1 tablespoon freshly squeezed orange juice
1 teaspoon sugar, or to taste
1 tablespoon minced fresh mint (do not substitute dried mint)

Taste how this blend of berries, fresh mint, and berry vinegar brings out the best in a refreshing summer fruit salad.

Place all ingredients, except mint, in a blender. Purée until smooth. Stir in mint. Chill. Stir before serving.

ADVANCE PREPARATION: This dressing will keep for a day in a tightly closed container in the refrigerator.

PER TABLESPOON: CALORIES 6 • FAT .04G • CHOL 0 • SODIUM .3MG

APPENDIX A

THE BASICS

Although all of the items in this chapter can be purchased in supermarkets, sometimes it is fun and certainly rewarding to make them from scratch. They can be made when time permits or when ingredients such as fresh basil are in plentiful supply and economical.

You'll be in for some pleasant surprises. Once you have made your own croutons (page 139), the packaged varieties just won't do. You'll be delighted to discover that Crème Fraîche (page 138) doesn't have to be sky-high in calories as well as price! The Zesty Mustard (page 142) is always in my refrigerator, and I often make extra to share with friends.

BAKED TORTILLA CHIPS

MAKES 24 CHIPS

4 six-inch or seven-inch
flour tortillas (white or
whole wheat)

These quick-to-prepare chips are an alternative to high-fat and high-sodium packaged chips. They are a great accompaniment to salads, especially a bean or green salad topped with Chunky Mexican Salsa Dressing (page 34).

Preheat oven to 400°F.

Using kitchen shears, cut each tortilla in half; then cut each half into 3 pie-shaped wedges. Arrange in a single layer on an ungreased baking sheet.

Bake in the preheated oven for 5 to 7 minutes or until crisp. (Chips will continue to become crisp as they cool.)

ADVANCE PREPARATION: The chips may be made in advance and stored in an airtight container at room temperature for a few days.

FOR 6 CHIPS: CALORIES 95 • FAT 1.8G • CHOL 0 • SODIUM NO DATA

VARIATION:
• lightly brush each side of the tortillas with
  1/4 teaspoon olive oil before cutting into wedges
  and baking (for 6 chips: calories 105)

BASIL PESTO

2 cups loosely packed
  fresh basil leaves
  (fresh is essential!)

1/4 cup pine nuts

1 teaspoon minced garlic

1/4 cup olive oil

1/4 teaspoon freshly
  ground black pepper,
  or to taste

On its own, Basil Pesto is one of the most flavorful sauces for pasta. But it also can be used to add a burst of flavor to salad dressings such as Pesto Vinaigrette (page 63) and Creamy Pesto Dressing (page 96). Or blend it into margarine or butter, adding a dash of lemon juice, to use as a flavorful spread for crusty bread to accompany your salads. To have it on hand when fresh basil is unavailable, make the pesto in advance and store it in your freezer.

Place the ingredients in a food processor; process until the mixture is a coarse purée, using a rubber scraper to push down the sides occasionally. Taste; adjust seasonings.

ADVANCE PREPARATION: The pesto may be made in advance. Spoon the mixture into a jar and pour a thin film of oil on top to prevent discoloration. Cover and refrigerate for up to 1 week. It may be used chilled for adding to salad dressings, but bring the pesto to room temperature before tossing with warm pasta. To freeze, spoon the mixture, in 2-tablespoon quantities, into foil-lined custard cups or muffin tins. Cover tightly with foil and freeze. Once frozen, remove the foil-wrapped packets and place in a freezer bag for up to 2 months. To use, allow to thaw in the refrigerator overnight or remove from the foil and thaw quickly in the microwave.

PER TABLESPOON: CALORIES **78** • FAT **7.9**G • CHOL **0** • SODIUM **6**MG

CRÈME FRAÎCHE

MAKES 1 CUP

1 cup half-and-half

2 tablespoons low-fat plain yogurt (must have active cultures, see page 13)

Crème fraîche purchased in the dairy department of your supermarket is pricey and high in fat (50 calories and 5.5 grams of fat per tablespoon). Here is the simplest method I've found for making a lower-cost and lower-fat version at home. Count on it as a creamy tart topping for desserts and fruit.

In a sterilized glass jar combine the half-and-half and yogurt. Cover tightly and shake for 2 minutes. Let stand at room temperature for 24 hours (on warm days, the cream will thicken faster).

Stir the cream, cover, and refrigerate. The flavor will intensify and the Crème Fraîche will continue to thicken. Stir before using.

ADVANCE PREPARATION: The Crème Fraîche will keep for 2 weeks in a tightly closed container in the refrigerator.

PER TABLESPOON: CALORIES 21 • FAT 1.8G • CHOL 6MG • SODIUM 7MG

Tip: Be certain to use a clean, sterilized glass container for your Crème Fraîche. For developing the culture, the room temperature may be between 65° and 90°F. If it is lower, the culture is slower to develop; if higher, the cream sours. A temperature of 80°F is just about perfect. Store the Crème Fraîche under refrigeration once the culture has developed. I have used this recipe successfully many times, but if you are uncomfortable allowing dairy products to stand at room temperature as the culture develops, purchase commercially prepared Crème Fraîche.

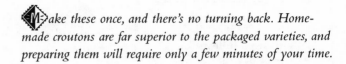

HERBED GARLIC CROUTONS

MAKES **1** CUP

1 tablespoon extra-virgin olive oil

1/4 teaspoon minced garlic

1/4 teaspoon dried basil

1/4 teaspoon dried oregano

1 cup 1/2-inch bread cubes (preferably whole wheat bread)

ake these once, and there's no turning back. Homemade croutons are far superior to the packaged varieties, and preparing them will require only a few minutes of your time.

In a small skillet, heat the olive oil over medium heat. Add the garlic, basil, and oregano. Stir for about 30 seconds to soften the herbs.

Stir in the bread cubes; stir until browned and crisp, 3 to 4 minutes. The croutons will become crisper as they cool.

ADVANCE PREPARATION: The croutons may be made a day in advance. Store in a tin at room temperature (they will become soggy in a plastic container). To recrisp, place on a baking sheet and heat for about 5 minutes at 350°F.

PER **1/4** CUP: CALORIES **50** • FAT **3.7**G • CHOL **0** • SODIUM **50**MG

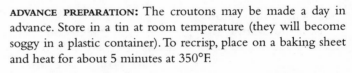

- for the basil and oregano, substitute other dried herbs such as thyme or tarragon; or substitute curry powder or chili powder, to taste
- croutons can also be made by toasting bread squares on a baking sheet at 350°F. until they are crispy and lightly browned, about 15 minutes

MAYONNAISE

MAKES 1 CUP

1/4 cup noncholesterol
egg product (at room
temperature)

2 tablespoons white rice
vinegar

2 teaspoons honey

1/8 teaspoon ground white
pepper

Pinch of dry mustard
powder

3/4 cup safflower oil
(at room temperature)

Mayonnaise is a smooth emulsion of eggs in oil to which
an acid, such as vinegar or lemon juice, and flavorings are
added.

Since homemade mayonnaise traditionally contains
uncooked eggs, sometimes known to cause salmonella food
poisoning, I experimented with pasteurized egg products to
eliminate these worries and was pleased with the results of
using noncholesterol and reduced-cholesterol egg products.

Using a blender, the procedure is simple. But note that
the emulsion will form only if the oil is added gradually,
while the blade is spinning.

This mayonnaise can be used in any of the salad
dressings calling for cholesterol-free mayonnaise. For a
simple dressing, use it alone; or it can be flavored with the
addition of herbs or citrus fruit zest.

Place all ingredients, except oil, in a blender. Blend until
smooth. Continue blending as you add the oil very slowly
in a steady stream, until the mixture is well mixed and
thick. Pour into a sterilized glass container.

ADVANCE PREPARATION: The mayonnaise will keep for 2 weeks
in a tightly closed container in the refrigerator.

PER TABLESPOON: CALORIES 95 • FAT 10G • CHOL 0 • SODIUM .1MG

MIXED FRUIT CHUTNEY

MAKES 1 1/2 CUPS

1/2 apple, peeled and diced
(about 1/2 cup)

4 dried apricot halves,
chopped (about 1/4 cup)

2 tablespoons freshly
squeezed lemon juice

2 tablespoons raisins

2 tablespoons dried
cranberries

1 tablespoon minced onion

1 tablespoon water

1 tablespoon white rice
vinegar

1 tablespoon light brown
sugar

1 teaspoon lemon zest

1/4 teaspoon cinnamon

1/8 teaspoon freshly
ground black pepper,
or to taste

Pinch ground cloves

Pinch allspice

1 pear, peeled, cored, and
diced

Here's a basic chutney recipe that can be varied by using other fresh, canned, or dried fruits. It can be served alone as an accompaniment or as a topping for fish or chicken. Although I often use commercially prepared chutney in the salad dressing recipes calling for it, this mixture can be substituted.

Place all ingredients, except the pear, in a medium-size saucepan. Cover and cook over medium heat for about 5 minutes.

Add the pear, cover, and cook for 5 minutes more, or until all fruits are softened.

ADVANCE PREPARATION: The chutney will keep for 4 days in a tightly closed container in the refrigerator.

PER TABLESPOON: CALORIES 16 • FAT .05G • CHOL 0 • SODIUM .6MG

VARIATIONS:

- for the apple, substitute 1/2 cup canned crushed pineapple; omit the lemon juice
- for the pear, substitute a peach
- add about 1/4 cup chopped walnuts or pecans, or sliced or slivered almonds

ZESTY MUSTARD

MAKES 1 CUP
1/2 cup dry mustard powder
1/2 cup white rice vinegar
1 egg
1/2 cup sugar

When time permits, I like to make this zesty but sweet mustard from scratch. It will provide a sweeter and less herbal flavor than Dijon, but it can be used in any of my dressing recipes that call for mustard. And, of course, it will also perk up your sandwiches!

In a small bowl, combine the mustard powder and vinegar; whisk to remove lumps. Cover and allow to stand at room temperature at least 4 hours or overnight.

When you are ready to make the mustard, heat water to a simmer in the bottom pan of a double boiler.

Pour the mustard-vinegar mixture into a blender. Blend with the egg and sugar until smooth.

Transfer the mixture to the top of a double boiler. Cook, stirring constantly, over simmering water until the mixture thickens to pudding consistency, 3 to 5 minutes.

Pour into a clean sterilized glass container and allow to come to room temperature; cover and refrigerate.

ADVANCE PREPARATION: The mustard will keep for 1 month in a tightly closed container in the refrigerator.

PER TABLESPOON: CALORIES 20 • FAT .4G • CHOL 13MG • SODIUM 41MG

VARIATION:
• for the whole egg, substitute 1/4 cup noncholesterol egg product or 2 egg whites

APPENDIX B

SUGGESTIONS FOR DRESSING USES

The introductions to many of the dressing recipes provide suggestions for their uses. Beyond that, the possibilities are endless. Here is a list of some of my favorite combinations to guide you in your creativity.

Dressings to Use for Greens and Vegetables

All of the "Oil and Vinegar Dressings" (chapter 1) and "Creamy Dressings" (chapter 2) are excellent on greens and vegetables. I also enjoy using the following from "Fruit Dressings" (chapter 3).

Berry Dressing with Poppy Seeds
Creamy Orange Curry Dressing
Honey and Yogurt Dressing
Honey-Lime Dressing

Lemon-Mint Dressing
Minted Chutney-Lime Sauce
Nectarine Dressing
Strawberry-Mint Vinaigrette

Dressings to Use for Marinating Vegetables

See the tips for marinating vegetables on page 26; select from this list for some particularly pleasing blends of flavors.

Oil and Vinegar Dressings

Balsamic Vinaigrette
Basic Vinaigrette
Basil-Sherry Vinaigrette

Dill Vinaigrette
Fat-Free Vinaigrette
Ginger-Soy Vinaigrette

Green French Dressing
Green Peppercorn Vinaigrette
Hot Pepper Vinaigrette
Italian Dressing
Lemon-Basil Vinaigrette
Parmesan Vinaigrette
Pesto Vinaigrette
Pistachio Vinaigrette
Raspberry-Walnut Vinaigrette

Roasted Garlic Vinaigrette
Savory Vinaigrette
Sesame-Orange Dressing
Sesame-Soy Dressing
Shallot and Caper Dressing
Sun-Dried Tomato–Rosemary
  Vinaigrette
Sweet and Sour Dressing
Tarragon Vinaigrette

CREAMY DRESSINGS

Creamy Lemon-Caper Dressing
Creamy Pesto Dressing

Creamy Tarragon-Dijon Dressing

DRESSINGS TO USE FOR GRAINS AND BEANS

Nearly all of the oil and vinegar dressings are compatible with grains and beans; however, I do not recommend the distinctly fruity-flavored dressings (Apple-Raspberry Vinaigrette, Grapefruit Vinaigrette, Papaya–Poppy Seed Vinaigrette, and Summer Peach Vinaigrette). Try these creamy dressings, too.

Creamy Balsamic Dressing
Creamy Goat Cheese Dressing
Creamy Herb Dressing
Creamy Italian Dressing
Creamy Lemon-Caper Dressing
Creamy Parmesan-Peppercorn Dressing
Creamy Pesto Dressing
Creamy Tarragon-Dijon Dressing

Hoisin Dressing
Honey-Dijon Dressing
Indonesian Peanut Dressing
Lemon Caesar Dressing
Parsley-Cucumber Dressing
Ranch Dressing
Ricotta-Chive Dressing

Dressings to Use for Fish and Shellfish

Some of my favorite entrée salads are composed of fish, shellfish, or chicken on a bed of greens. You'll enjoy the flavorful combinations using any of the "Oil and Vinegar Dressings" (chapter 1) and "Creamy Dressings" (chapter 2). For variety, also try these recipes from "Fruit Dressings" (chapter 3).

Creamy Orange Curry Dressing
Lemon-Mint Dressing
Minted Chutney-Lime Sauce

Nectarine Dressing
Strawberry-Mint Vinaigrette

Dressings to Use for Duck

Duck is most compatible with fruity dressings such as the following:

Oil and Vinegar Dressings

Marmalade Vinaigrette
Orange Vinaigrette

Papaya–Poppy Seed Vinaigrette

Fruit Dressings

Creamy Orange Curry Dressing

Dressings to Use for Turkey

Sometimes I enjoy creating a chef's salad with strips of turkey arranged on a bed of greens drizzled with one of these dressings:

Oil and Vinegar Dressings

Cranberry-Maple Vinaigrette

Savory Vinaigrette

CREAMY DRESSINGS

 Apricot–Yogurt Dressing

DRESSINGS TO USE FOR LAMB

OIL AND VINEGAR DRESSINGS

 Basil–Sherry Vinaigrette   Honey–Mint Dressing
 Chutney Vinaigrette

CREAMY DRESSINGS

 Apricot–Yogurt Dressing   Cucumber–Dill Dressing
 Chutney–Yogurt Dressing   Parsley–Cucumber Dressing
 Creamy Lemon–Basil Dressing

FRUIT DRESSINGS

 Minted Chutney–Lime Sauce

DRESSINGS TO USE FOR PORK

OIL AND VINEGAR DRESSINGS

 Apple–Raspberry Vinaigrette   Italian Dressing
 Apricot–Sesame Dressing   Orange Vinaigrette
 Chutney Vinaigrette

CREAMY DRESSINGS

    Apple–Celery Seed Dressing

DRESSINGS TO USE FOR BEEF

I think beef is best served with a highly flavored herbal dressing or one containing tomatoes.

OIL AND VINEGAR DRESSINGS

Chopped Vegetable Vinaigrette

Fat-Free Vinaigrette

Green French Dressing

Green Peppercorn Vinaigrette

Herbed Tomato Sauce

Italian Dressing

Mesquite Tomato Dressing

Paprika Vinaigrette

Southwestern Dried Chili Pepper
    Dressing

CREAMY DRESSINGS

Creamy Italian Dressing

Creamy Lemon-Basil Dressing

Parsley-Cucumber Dressing

Ranch Dressing

Ricotta-Chive Dressing

DRESSINGS TO USE FOR PASTA

Since pasta on its own is quite bland, the dressing will give your pasta salad its personality. For the best flavor, serve your mixture of pasta and vegetables at room temperature rather than straight from the refrigerator. It is usually best to toss in the dressing just before serving.

OIL AND VINEGAR DRESSINGS

Balsamic Vinaigrette
Basic Vinaigrette
Basil-Sherry Vinaigrette
Chopped Vegetable Vinaigrette
Dill Vinaigrette
Fat-Free Vinaigrette
Garden Salad Dressing
Green French Dressing
Green Peppercorn Vinaigrette
Herbed Anchovy Dressing
Herbed Tomato Sauce
Honey–Poppy Seed Dressing
Hot Pepper Vinaigrette
Italian Dressing
Lemon-Basil Vinaigrette

Mesquite Tomato Dressing
Parmesan Vinaigrette
Pesto Vinaigrette
Roasted Garlic Vinaigrette
Roasted Sweet Red Pepper Dressing
Savory Vinaigrette
Sesame-Soy Dressing
Shallot and Caper Dressing
Southwestern Dried Chili Pepper Dressing
Sun-Dried Tomato–Rosemary Vinaigrette
Tarragon Vinaigrette
Vegetable Juice Vinaigrette

CREAMY DRESSINGS

Creamy Balsamic Dressing
Creamy Herb Dressing
Creamy Italian Dressing
Creamy Lemon-Basil Dressing
Creamy Lemon-Caper Dressing
Creamy Parmesan-Peppercorn Dressing
Creamy Peanut Dressing
Creamy Pesto Dressing
Creamy Tarragon-Dijon Dressing

Creamy Tomato Dressing
Cucumber-Dill Dressing
Greek Feta Cheese Dressing
Honey-Dijon Dressing
Lemon Caesar Dressing
Parsley-Cucumber Dressing
Ranch Dressing
Ricotta-Chive Dressing

Dressings to Use for Fruit

Most often I use "Fruit Dressings" (chapter 3) when I plan my fruit salads. For a change of pace, the fruity-flavored "Oil and Vinegar Dressings" (chapter 1) and "Creamy Dressings" (chapter 2) can also be used to turn a bowl of fruit into something special.

Oil and Vinegar Dressings

Apple-Raspberry Vinaigrette
Apricot-Sesame Dressing
Caribbean Dressing
Chutney Vinaigrette
Cranberry-Maple Vinaigrette
Gingered Lime Vinaigrette
Gingered Plum Vinaigrette
Grapefruit Vinaigrette
Hazelnut Vinaigrette

Honey-Mint Dressing
Honey–Poppy Seed Dressing
Maple-Cranberry Vinaigrette
Marmalade Vinaigrette
Orange Vinaigrette
Papaya–Poppy Seed Vinaigrette
Pineapple-Sesame Vinaigrette
Raspberry-Walnut Vinaigrette
Summer Peach Vinaigrette

Creamy Dressings

Apple–Celery Seed Dressing
Apricot-Yogurt Dressing
Chutney-Yogurt Dressing

Creamy Curried Grapefruit
  Dressing
Curried Yogurt Dressing

INDEX